Startup CMO

A Field Guide to Scaling up Your Company's Marketing Function

Matt Blumberg, Nick Badgett and Holly Enneking

Bolster Network

Contents

Foreword

Scott Dorsey

As a first-time tech founder and CEO at ExactTarget, one phrase kept ringing through my head: "I don't know what I don't know." Even with 10+ years of business experience and a freshly minted MBA degree, I had so many blind spots having never built software, raised venture capital or even led a multi-functional organization. Filling in these gaps took many years and lots of trial and error.

One of my gap-filling strategies was to learn from other CEOs going through similar highs and lows of scaling their company. On this journey, I was fortunate to meet Matt Blumberg. As CEO of Return Path, Matt was building a high growth company in the same digital marketing industry as me. I was impressed by his leadership, strategic thinking, and commitment to helping other entrepreneurs. We became fast friends and we both looked forward to learning from one another.

Matt was always gracious and willing to take my call or have dinner together. Our conversations covered every topic imaginable from leadership to board management to strategic partnerships to international expansion. My advice to entrepreneurs and leaders––build your peer network and spend time developing and nurturing these relationships. While board members and advisors are an important source of knowledge, learning from peers can be invaluable.

One of the highlights of my relationship with Matt was when we were both invited to the White House to witness President Obama signing the Jumpstart our Business Startups Act (or JOBS Act) in April of 2012. With bi-partisan support, the law opened up crowdfunding for startups and streamlined the IPO path. ExactTarget had just gone public two weeks prior so I knew the benefits that the JOBS Act would bring to entrepreneurs. But what I didn't know in April 2012 was that the event would foreshadow my relationship with Matt and how we would work together supporting entrepreneurs and startup ecosystems.

Fast forward to 2020. We are facing unprecedented challenges in the world and the need for innovation and leadership has never been greater. CEOs and functional leaders need tools and resources to accelerate their learning curves and the learning curves of those around them. Speed of learning, thought, and action are more important now than ever. This is why I am so excited about Matt's latest book, *Startup CXO*.

Startup CXO provides a comprehensive field guide to starting and scaling tech companies. Really, the information is super helpful to any company. It provides a "book within a book" framework to enable and empower readers to jump into any section as needed. And it's written by practitioners who provide tons of tangible advice and actionable insights. By reading this book, I believe that leaders will be better equipped to build great companies and anticipate what's around every corner.

In my view, the best CEOs have a grasp of all functions. They can go a mile wide and a couple inches deep. They hire A+ talent and build a culture that brings out the very best in people. They understand how Sales and Marketing fit together, they value HR, Finance, and Legal and understand their interdependencies, they have a clear vision for how Product and Engineering fit together, they know how to be aggressive and how to manage risk, and so much more.

So, *Startup CXO* is an amazing resource for CEOs but also for functional leaders and professionals at any stage of their career. The best functional leaders and professionals understand that cross-functional teamwork is everything. It's so important to have insight and empathy for how other areas of the organization operate. The big picture is needed to see how all of the puzzle pieces fit together.

I feel so lucky that through our venture studio, High Alpha, I have the opportunity to work with Matt and his leadership team as we build

Bolster––a talent marketplace for startup and scaleup tech companies. We are living and applying the concepts and lessons contained in this very book!

My wish for you is that reading *Startup CXO* minimizes your "I don't know what I don't know" list; that it accelerates your development, your curiosity, your ability to ask the right questions, and helps you surround yourself with the right talent. My wish is that you dream big, lead with purpose and integrity, and master your craft. I hope—and believe—that *Startup CXO* will be a helpful companion for you on your company-building journey.

Good luck!

Scott Dorsey

Managing Partner – High Alpha

November 2020

Update for 2024 Edition

I was delighted to hear that Matt and his leadership team at Bolster are breaking out *Startup CXO* into a series of enhanced mini-books to cover the "big 5" functions in a startup -- Finance, HR, Sales, Marketing, and Product/Tech. Each of these mini books provides the reader with a streamlined view of the critical elements of a single leadership function in a startup and highlights some of the best thinking around how to hire and lead teams. This book is power-packed with actionable insights that will serve as a valuable resource as startup teams scale.

Enjoy!

Scott Dorsey

Managing Partner – High Alpha

August 2024

Introduction

Matt Blumberg

In 2020 we sold Return Path, a company we had grown from a startup to over 500 employees over two decades. I documented the CEO journey in *Startup CEO: A Field Guide to Scaling Up Your Business*, but after publishing *Startup CEO* I was left with the nagging feeling that it wasn't enough to only help CEOs excel, because starting and scaling a business is a collective effort. What about the other critical leadership functions that are needed to grow a company? If you're leading HR, or Finance, or Marketing, or any key function inside a startup, what resources are available to you? What should you be thinking about? What does "great" look like for your function? What challenges lurk around the corner as you scale your function that you might not be focused on today? What are your fellow executives focused on in their own departments, and how can you best work together? If you're a CEO who has never managed all these functions before, what should you be looking for when you hire and manage all these people? If you're an aspiring executive, from entry-level to manager to director, what do you need to think about as you grow your career and develop your skills? And if you're a Board client or investor, what scorecard or metrics are you using to ensure your companies and investments are achieving greatness?

A number of my Return Path colleagues and I founded Bolster shortly after exiting Return Path and we started thinking about a new book as a sequel or companion to *Startup CEO.* That was the origin of *Startup CXO: A Field Guide to Scaling Up Your Company's Critical Functions and Teams. Startup CXO* ended up being a "book of books," with eight separate, detailed sections, one for each major function inside a company. Each section was composed of several discrete short chapters outlining the key playbooks for each functional leadership role in the company. Because it covered CFOs, CMOs, CPOs, etc.--we landed on "Startup CXO" as the name. As a field guide, *Startup CXO* was massive—over 600 pages and 132 chapters and while we think the content is relevant to the entire leadership team, we recognize that a more focused book on each function is also something people need. The result is the book you have here, *Startup CMO: A Field Guide to Scaling up Your Company's Marketing Function*, which is written for the current or aspiring Chief Marketing Officer who wants to know how to scale their function, wants to know what "great" looks like, and wants to work effectively with other members of the organization. As an added benefit, this book is shorter, easier to carry, and cheaper.

While the content in this book is largely the same as *Startup CXO*, we updated it and added several chapters on "How to Hire a CMO," and "Marketing as a Partner: Collaborating with the Rest of the Leadership Team." We also moved the chapter on Fractional work from *Startup CXO* to this book so that all of the relevant CMO information is in one book.

One major change we should note is a reflection of society: when we wrote *Startup CXO*, the pandemic was just underway and neither us nor anyone else could have predicted the impact globally, much less the drastic impact on startups and entrepreneurship. The impact of the pandemic on the world of work, in how business is conducted is well-known, from the great resignation to the permanence of remote work and hybrid models, but in the world of entrepreneurship the impact is less well-known. For example, in 2020 we wrote that "America's 'startup revolution' continues to gather steam" and noted that there are "increasing numbers of venture capital investors, seed funds, and accelerators supporting increasing numbers of entrepreneurial ventures." Today the world has changed, and while startup activity is still quite high, we are seeing more down-rounds, re-pricings, and recaps as venture capitalists are de-risking their investments. We're seeing expanding deal timelines and a focus on governance and accountability. Founders are likely to be operating under a microscope with less leeway, and with more scrutiny on management accountability and structures ensuring performance-based compensation. What that means for today's founders is that they need to develop a great organization right out of the gate, and that's where *Startup CMO* will come in handy.

While there are a number of books in the marketplace about CEOs and leadership, and some about individual functional disciplines (lots of books on the topic of Sales, the topic of Product Development, and the like), there are very few books that are practical how-to guides for any individual function, and that is where this series of "mini books" can help guide startup and scaleup teams. Each book in this series will serve as a how-to guide for a given executive, and taken together, the series will be a good how-to guide for startup executive teams in general. The five books are:

Finance and Administration
People and Human Resources
Marketing
Sales
Product and Engineering

We are starting with these "big five," but we may come back later and add to the series with Customer Success, Privacy, Business Development, and Operations, the other sections of *Startup CXO*.

This book carries my name as its principal author, and although I'm writing parts of it and editing it, I'm not THE author, I'm AN author. Nick Badgett and Holly Enneking have been involved in marketing at Return Path and Bolster and they are the principal authors and the ones who have the experience, credibility, and expertise to share something of value with others in the Marketing function. This material was also read and edited by additional CMOs we know.

One caveat. Although this book is being written by Nick, Holly, and me, it is not meant to be the Return Path story. We all have 10–30 years of experience working at multiple companies of different sizes and at different stages and in different sectors on which we are drawing. It's also not the story of Bolster, the new company that a number of us started during the pandemic in 2020. The book is based on our experience mostly in U.S.-based tech or tech-enabled services businesses, and more from the perspective of B2B than B2C, though inclusive of both. A few notes on language. We realize that not every leadership role in a startup is actually a "C"-level role. Sometimes the most senior person running a functional department is an SVP, a VP, a "head of," or even a Director or Manager. But Startup Functional Leader is a lousy title for a book. Regardless of title, we wrote with the most senior person responsible for the Marketing function in mind. Another point on terminology is that we use the words startup and scaleup in the book without precise revenue-based or employee-count-based definitions, but you should assume that startups are smaller companies, whereas scaleups are ones that have already reached some meaningful level of critical mass. We also use terms like "executive team," "leadership team," "C-suite," and "executive committee" interchangeably to refer to a company's senior-most group of leaders. Finally, we frequently refer to the concept of an "operating system." I talked about this at length in my earlier book, Startup CEO, but basically, it means––whether for a person, a team, or a company––the collection of meeting and communication routines and operating practices that form the cadence of a team's work.

Although the book is focused on the CMO role, there are insights for others in an organization. So, if you're a CEO, you could gain some additional insight into why something is not working in your Marketing organization––and understand how and what to change to create success in your Marketing team. I also have a "CEO-to-CEO Advice" section where I share my thoughts on what "great" looks like for the CMO, signs that your CMO isn't scaling, and how I engage with the CMO. I believe (and hope!) that CEOs, Board members, and investors can quickly get an overview and understanding of the CMO function by reading the "CEO-to-CEO Advice" chapter.

If you are a CMO or aspiring to become one, I hope this book speaks to you and inspires you in some way––that it's a playbook for something meaningful to you. If you're a CEO, maybe it will help you figure out who to hire or how to more effectively manage your CMO by telling you what "great" looks like for a CMO. If you're already a CMO in a startup, maybe it will help you focus on some aspect of your role you hadn't thought about yet. If you're an aspiring leader, maybe it will give you some insight into the kinds of steps you need to take in order to grow your career. Whichever persona you are, on behalf of me, Nick, and Holly, we hope you gain some insight, and we thank you for reading *Startup CMO: A Field Guide to Scaling up Your Company's Marketing Function.*

I. WELCOME TO THE EXECUTIVE TEAM

Matt Blumberg

Bolster Network

The Nature of a CXO's Role

I was struck by something as I read over the nearly complete manuscript of *Startup CXO* for the first time: each CXO believes that their part of the business is the most important part. And they make a compelling set of arguments:

Shawn: If you don't have a good product, you don't have a business.

Anita: If you don't have revenues, you don't have a business.

Ken: If you don't develop the ecosystem, you don't have a business.

Nick: If you don't generate market opportunities, you don't have a business.

George: If you don't create exceptional customer experiences, you don't have a business.

Cathy: If you don't recruit, train, and develop the right people, you don't have a business.

Jack: If you don't have the cash, you don't have a business.

Dennis: If you don't bake privacy in at the beginning, you don't have a business.

We had a debate years ago at a Return Path Board meeting as to whether we were a sales-driven business or a product-driven business—and more important, whether we should be one or the other.

Two of our Board members, both of whom I respect tremendously, were anchoring the different points of view, Scott Petry, on the product side, talking about how successful Apple was at getting customers to camp out overnight to be the first ones to buy the newest iThing; and Greg Sands, on the sales side, talking about how successful Oracle was at getting product into the hands of customers. I took a devil's advocate point of view in the conversation, true to our operating philosophy at Return Path, which was that HR/People was the most important function because we were a people-driven business.

So, who is right? Are the best companies sales-driven, product-driven, people-driven, or something else? Which of the CXO's functions is the most important? My answer is—they all are important, just in different ways, at different times, and in different combinations. While it's the CEO's job to balance the functions out—to figure out which lever to pull at which time, it's the CXO's job to be at the ready when their lever is pulled. And that gets to the important question of what the nature of a CXO role is, and why those roles can be tricky. CXOs have three principal jobs that they must keep in balance at all times, although there is a clear priority in my mind of the three jobs.

CXOs are first and foremost members of the company's Executive Team. They must, must, must put that team, understanding of the different functions, and the relationships on it at the top of their agenda. They shouldn't show up on the team only advocating for their own team. CEOs must insist on that behavior and mentality. Without it, a company simply can't function sustainably. This concept is one that we have always called the First Team concept, and it's articulated very eloquently by Patrick Lencioni in a number of his books, particularly in *The Five Dysfunctions of a Team* and *The Advantage*. As members of the Executive Team, all CXOs are accountable to each other for the success of the business as a whole and must partner with each other to achieve that success.

CXOs are also the head of their respective functional departments. They must carry the flag of their team and wave it proudly throughout the organization, especially when working with their teams. They are the functional role model, the functional mentor, and the functional decision-maker for the people on their functional team. To be an effective leader, they must be The Quintessential X (sales professional, engineer, marketer, etc.).

Finally, CXOs are company leaders. They are role models for company values. They should always be on alert for things that are going well or going poorly around them. Things that need attention or recognition. Situations that need calming down. Guests who are sitting unattended in the office lobby. Delivery people who need a check signed and who need to be tipped. Putting the new bottle of water onto the water cooler. You get the idea. Company leaders have the actual and moral authority to step outside of their departments and handle things as they need to be handled, regardless of which employees are involved.

Scaling a CMO

Congratulations, you just got promoted from Director of Marketing to CMO! You're now in charge of a whole functional department, you now report to the CEO, you're now on the Executive Committee. You have a whole bunch of direct reports that either represent the team you used to lead or yesterday were your peers and you have now reached the pinnacle of your career in the Marketing organization. The only other ways to grow your career vertically are to lead your function at a larger and larger company, or to become a CEO. Wow!

That feeling of euphoria is wonderful. I remember having it when I worked at MovieFone and became the head of marketing and product management instead of just the "Internet guy." It definitely led to a nice celebratory night out in Manhattan with friends.

But then, the reality set in the next morning. Uh oh. I've never done this job before. Maybe I know how to do 25% of it. I'm only 26 years old. Is anyone going to respect me? I have so much to learn. Can I fake it? How on earth did I find myself here? This phenomenon is called the Imposter Syndrome, and it's totally normal. In fact, if you grow your career quickly, it would be weird not to have at least a touch of it.

The good news is, you're not the first person to be promoted to an executive role for the first time (and of course you're not the last, either). Every single executive, at any company, had their first executive role at some point. While there's some credence to the expression "fake it till you make it," there's a more methodical approach you can take to scaling yourself as a CMO—or if you're the CEO, to helping your new CMO scale. Think of the journey in three steps that can be taken in any order.

First, master the tactics. You need to understand all of the things that happen in your department. Some, you will know well because they're the ones you've done over time. Some you won't know at all. Make sure you do a complete inventory of the functional competencies for your role and all the roles reporting to you. Depending on how organized your company is with job descriptions and what's often known as a RACI (responsible-accountable-consulted-informed) analysis, this may be as easy as pulling something off the shelf and having a series of meetings with the people on your team to walk you through what they do. If your company isn't that organized, you may want to take the opportunity to proactively build that kind of functional competency/RACI list for everything in your team. That is no small exercise, but it's one that will pay back massive dividends. As one of my long-time colleagues, Anita Absey, says, "What gets measured gets managed." I'd add to that: if you don't know something even exists, you can't begin to measure it, let alone manage it!

Second, form your strategic approach. Every single function in a company has tactical and transactional elements to it—and every single function can be ONLY tactical if you let it. That's the lowest common denominator. HR can be about benefits and payroll. Sales can be about pipeline management and closing deals. Marketing can be about blog posts and SEO. A transactional focus is especially true of corporate functions like HR and Finance, but it's true of all functions. But just as every function has its tactical elements that must be attended to, every function CAN be strategic. As you settle into your new role, and as you grow into the role of senior executive and learn the First Team lesson of putting the needs of the business before the needs of your department, you will be able to start thinking more holistically about the business and how your department fits into it, so when your CEO pulls the lever that indicates they need your team to step up and lead, to be strategic on some topic, you are ready. What does it mean to be strategic vs. tactical? It's the difference between eating what's on your plate and planning out next week's menu. What are the ways in which the Marketing organization can produce competitive differentiation for the business? What are the frameworks that will guide your decision-making about resource allocation or prioritization? How can you best support the other departments in the company? Those are the kinds of things you need to master in step 2. As my colleague Dave Wilby once said about one of the teams he was managing, "We have to figure out how to be the nose, not the tail."

Finally, look around the corner to see what's next for you and for your team. Senior executives constantly need to be toggling between different execution and planning horizons. You need to make your goals this quarter, and to make them, you have to hit daily or weekly activity metrics and milestones. But what about next quarter? Or next year? Or what happens if your company doubles in size in the next six months and is set to double again? Start by revisiting that functional competency/RACI list from step 1 and stress-test every element of it. Ask yourself, what must be true of this line item when the company is twice its current size? While you have to develop and scale as a leader—with all that goes into that in terms of soft skills—the only way to scale yourself as a CMO is to understand what great looks like for your role at the next stage of the company's life, and make sure you don't get there after your company needs you to.

All three of these steps—mastering the tactics of your department, forming your strategic approach, and understanding what's next—are things you may be able to do on your own to a point. That said, they will all go more quickly and with a higher probability of success if you engage your CEO, your Head of HR, members of your Board, or outside mentors or coaches to assist you on your journey.

II. CHIEF MARKETING OFFICER

Nick Badgett, Holly Enneking, and Matt Blumberg

Chief Marketing Officer

What Is Marketing, Really?

Here's the thing, everybody thinks they're a marketer. Everybody. Whether they ever read a book on marketing or not, whether they ever took a course on marketing or not, everybody *thinks* they know something about marketing. And really, who can blame them? We're all marketed to throughout the course of our lives, from childhood to death and we all have opinions on what we like, what moves us to purchase something, and what turns us off. We all have brands that we follow, admire, or loathe. Maybe it's the visual identity that you gravitate toward and that tee shirt you love. Maybe it's a message that really nails it. It could be an advertisement or jingle, an email you received, something you saw on social media or TV, or the way you feel when you're in a store or on a website. Maybe it's the product itself. Regardless, we all have exposure to good, and maybe not so good, marketing.

The beauty of marketing lies in the sheer variety of approaches, methods, and mediums at your disposal, and it's also what makes it challenging. Marketing is unique and different to each one of us, and we all have opinions. And as a marketer, you're sure to hear them. How you respond to these opinions, requests, and ideas (lots of ideas) can often steer you on or off course. As a startup CMO your main problem is not going to be that there's nothing to do, or that you don't have any ideas but just the opposite: you'll have more ideas than you can possibly vet and more things on your plate than you can possibly complete.

Why Are French Fries Like Marketing?

> My friend Seth has a theory about life called the French Fry Theory. The theory is simple—"you always have room for one more fry." It's pretty spot-on, if you think about it. Fries are so tasty, and so relatively small (most of the time), that it's easy to just keep eating, and eating, and eating them.
>
> I've always thought that the French Fry Theory can be applied to many things, usually other food items. However, I came up with a new application today: Marketing.
>
> So why are French fries like Marketing? You can always do one more thing. One more press release. One more piece of collateral. One more page on the corporate website. One more newsletter. Trade show. Webinar. Research study. Ad. Search engine placement. Vendor. System. Speech. Take your pick.
>
> The world we operate in is so dynamic that marketing (when done well) is nearly impossible to ever feel like you're completely on top of. There's always more to be done, and the trick to doing it well is knowing when to say "no" as much as when to charge into something.
>
> My hat's off to twenty-first-century online-industry marketers. To bring this analogy back to its starting point...their plates are full!
>
> **Matt Blumberg,** *Executive Chair, Bolster*

What you need as a startup CMO is a framework to organize and prioritize your efforts so you work on the tasks that will make a big impact. Marketing has evolved to include production, sales philosophy, relationship and customer focus, social, digital, and marketing technology. We expect marketing to continue to evolve and, as CMO, your responsibility is to identify and evaluate new tools, take on new responsibilities, and manage big expectations. Your ability to leverage data and report on marketing return on investment will prove to your company the value of marketing efforts, and the rest of the C-suite will take notice, too.

So, what is Marketing, really? It is the process or technique of promoting, selling, and distributing a product or service as Merriam-Webster defines it. But we'd like to suggest another way to look at it, a perspective that we've learned throughout our careers in startups. We believe that marketing has three primary responsibilities:

1. Build and maintain the company brand.
2. Generate demand for sales.
3. Support the company culture.

When it comes down to it, most everything that we do in marketing can be attributed to supporting one of these primary responsibilities, sometimes more than one, sometimes all three.

Where to Start

Where to start can be daunting, but it can be simplified if you look at it through the lens of the three primary responsibilities outlined earlier. Focus on building the brand first because if you don't have a brand or a perspective on your brand or if you don't have the narrative or you don't have values or if you can't articulate your culture, then you don't have any reasonable way to go to the market. Imagine the following conversation:

Potential customer: What's the name of your company?
You: We haven't figured that out yet.
Potential customer: What is it that you're selling?
You: We're working on it.
Potential customer: What's the price of your product?
You: We don't know yet.
Potential customer: Why should I bother with you, your company, or your product?
You: We're good people. Trust us. We'll get there.

As excited as you might be to get out in the market and start selling your product, if you don't have clear thinking—from everyone in the company—about your brand and all that it entails, you'll never have the consistency and discipline to gain any traction in the market. You may be able to sell a few products, to generate some revenues, but without the brand you'll stall and you won't be able to scale, much less create a sustainable business.

Building and Maintaining a Brand

It's probably worth discussing what brand means because if you ask ten people what "brand" means, you'll likely get ten different answers. That's a problem for any company but especially for startups. Yes, the brand is your logo, your wordmark, your company name, your messaging, and other obvious graphics and phrases. It's also much more. It's the associations and the way a person feels when interacting with your brand, product, or service. At ExactTarget, we used to say that your brand is the sum of the conversations about it. We like to look at brand this way because it turns the brand from something that is static, that is "viewed" into something that is dynamic, something that engages people.

When we first started at Return Path, they were not a startup anymore but well on their way to scaling up with 400 employees and $80M + in revenue. One of the first things we did was a brand refresh, which is fairly common when new marketing leadership is brought in. In fact, that might be why a new marketing leader is brought in—to break up the old way of thinking and generate some fresh ideas. For us, it was time, and we had alignment and support from our CEO, our Board, and leadership team. We knew the brand was tired and needed a refresh, plus the business had evolved over the years, we had created new business units, and we wanted our brand to reflect that evolution. We worked with an agency over the course of a few months to support the initiative, revamping everything from the logo (which hadn't changed for more than 15 years!), to the color palette, to design elements, to the brand voice. It was rewarding and successful and a lot of work. However, we had the benefit of an already established and reputable brand to work with, we had the building blocks in place, and we just needed a visual refresh. But what about creating a brand?

You might think that creating a brand starts with a company name and logo, something a lot of people spend a great deal of time and energy perfecting. But before you spend any effort doing that, we'd suggest you work on creating a brand perspective. Without that strategy, you'll never be able to facilitate the conversations around your brand from partners, customers, and employees. Start by asking yourself and your colleagues general questions that help you understand how to shape what you want to be as a company, as a brand. Who are we? Who is our audience? What is our industry, and where do we fit in? How would we describe the personality and attributes of our desired brand? What value will we provide our audience? What do we do? How and why do we do it?

On the surface, these questions are simple, but answering them takes a lot of thought and you'll get better results if you ask a wide range of people to weigh in. You'll also get better results if you take time to let all the ideas sink in. This is not a 15-minute conversation or a short survey that you send out broadly, and it's not something that can get done in one meeting. But, if you have answers from a diverse group of people on these questions, you'll find that several recurring themes or concepts emerge. Those themes and concepts form the basis for your brand strategy. Notice that I didn't suggest that the CMO or marketing lead "creates" the brand strategy and then seeks to get buy-in from others in the company. That's the wrong way to approach it, that's a top-down, I'm-smarter-than-you approach that will never be effective.

We used this exact methodical approach when we were developing the brand for our new startup, Bolster. All of the company founders participated in the exercise, guided by our partners at High Alpha Venture Studio. We derived five concepts resulting from examining our company name and synonyms: (1) Support and Strengthen; (2) Boost and Energize; (3) Connection; (4) Grow and Thrive; and (5) Fast and Disruptive. From there, we explored visual representations of the concepts and ultimately, we were able to whittle down the concepts to two that will be the foundation for our brand strategy: (1) Support and Strengthen and (2) Connection. We had a few rounds of exploring these visual representations, which we used to select our logo and wordmark.

bolster logo

We also used the same approach five years earlier when we needed to develop a name, logo, and other elements for a new non-profit we were spinning out from Return Path. The "Returnship" or "Return to Work" program helped people (mostly Moms but some Dads) re-enter the workforce after taking a break for caregiving with a paid internship reinforced by training and networking, and when the program became a standalone entity, it needed a clear identity. Our brand team started to create the new identity by creating an overall framework.

The new name and brand should:

- Maintain a connection with Return Path;

- Not be gendered;

- Be inclusive;

- Feel aspirational and achievable.

After multiple brainstorming sessions and developing proposals around a variety of names, the founders selected the eventual winner: Path Forward.

When establishing your brand, collaborating broadly across the organization is key. You can achieve that by having each founding team member participate, or by collecting ideas and input from key stakeholders in the company. This collaboration can be extremely valuable in generating creative ideas and creating alignment around the eventual brand. It won't just be owned by the CEO or CMO, dictating to the rest of the company what the brand will be, but becomes a shared creation driven by the input and engagement of a broader base of the company. This level of collaboration is invaluable, and reflective of similar approaches in other parts of the business, including product development, creating company values, business development, and more. There won't always be unanimous agreement, but everyone is able to provide input, agree or disagree, commit, and move on.

5

Generating Demand for Sales

There are many different personas that fit today's CMO, but we like to think of the key ones as brand, growth, product, and influence. Some people would argue that the growth CMO is the most sought-after persona in today's business environment (for both B2B and B2C). After all, marketing—if done right—is no longer a cost center, but a revenue center. Demand generation, or growth, is the set of sales and marketing tools, approaches, systems, and programs that generate interest for your product or service. They are the things that nurture prospects into customers and retain those customers over time. Unlike the traditional marketer who is measured by the number of leads generated, the demand generation marketer is measured by their contribution to revenue.

That sounds logical, doesn't it? That a growth CMO is measured by their contribution to revenue? But there's a lot that goes into figuring out how demand leads to revenue. John Wanamker, considered by some to be a pioneer of marketing, is credited with coining the phrase "Half the money I spend on advertising is wasted; the trouble is I don't know which half." Good demand generation is anchored by good data, and good data will allow you to understand your marketing and sales cycles. Good data also helps you identify and refine your ideal buyer and understand what's working and what's not working. You need good data to make informed decisions about marketing investment and without a rigorous, comprehensive way to collect, analyze, and act on data, you're left with nothing more than hope and luck.

Market Research

So, where do you start with demand generation? We'd suggest starting with early market research so you can get some solid data. You can't determine your demand generation strategy without better understanding your company's target market and understanding how customers will react to your product or service. The information you collect during market research will also help your business with product design, improve the user experience and craft your messaging. Don't be intimidated by the word "research." We know it sounds academic and conjures up thoughts of statistics, but there are multiple ways to perform market research, there are agencies that specialize in the craft, and there are numerous books focused on this topic alone. The key is to start doing it, and once you do that you'll build a competency in market research and it will drive everything that you'll do in marketing. So, don't wait on this task!

At Bolster, we decided to tackle market research by following the principles in Ash Maurya's seminal startup product book, *Running Lean*. We started by conducting one-to-one interviews with our defined audiences and, in some cases, had two team members present to make sure nothing slipped through the cracks. We first established personas for our audiences. Think about a persona as a collection of attributes (beliefs, values) that are similar within a group of people but different from other groups. In our case we came up with three different personas. Then, we conducted over 100 interviews with those personas, and we are still conducting interviews as we are writing this. The first round of interviews we called the "problem interviews" and our aim was to identify our early adopters and learn about their biggest problems and how they currently solve them. The next round of interviews we called the "solution interviews" because we wanted feedback on our proposed solutions to those problems. And what we were really trying to determine was the smallest solution that would work, the minimum viable product (MVP).

For both problem and solution rounds, we found it extremely important to remain objective. We began each interview by stating our hypothesis on the problem or proposed solution and either asked respondents how they currently solve that problem today or asked them to respond to our proposed solution. Then we waited. We didn't prod them for a response, we didn't rephrase the questions. We just sat back and listened. By listening, we mean *really* listening, and it is the key to making this a valuable exercise. We used a script to make sure that we're staying on task, but we also allowed ourselves to vary off script in order to truly listen to what our respondents had to say. We documented our results, reviewed all of the responses, and discussed our findings during our weekly strategy meeting. We continue to conduct these interviews, refining what we want feedback on as we go, and we anticipate that these will not stop for some time.

Competitive Intelligence

We probably should also share that we conducted a fair amount of competitive research prior to starting our interviews. We documented every player even remotely close to what we're doing, and captured every piece of applicable information we could to compare to. It really helped us hone in on our primary competitors, complementary players, and gave us a lens into several elements of the business that hadn't originally occurred to us before. Competitive intelligence is not the sole domain of marketing, and there are others in the company—people who are in Product or who are customer-facing—who have insight on competitors, the market, and trends.

Technology

There is no question that technology has changed marketing. Some people say that marketing hasn't really changed but that technology has changed marketing, and there's a lot of truth to that. A 2015 industry report listed 1,876 vendors in the marketing technology (martech) space but by 2023 the number had increased to over 11,000 martech solutions! Obviously, you won't be able to evaluate even 1 percent of the potential vendors out there, so where do you start? It's daunting, but I'd suggest starting simple and growing your tech stack as your business needs change. There are a set of requirements for all businesses that you'll need to address, such as budget and B2B versus B2C, but there are a handful of areas that you'll need a solution for early on:

- Customer Relationship Management (CRM)

- Content Management System (CMS)

- Advertising and Search Engine Optimization (SEO)

- Email

- Project management/collaboration

- Social

- Analytics and reporting

A good CRM system is your foundation and it's what you should start with, regardless of your industry or offering. This is especially true if you have limited resources. Some of the more robust CRM tools today have marketing automation, social, SEO, landing pages, analytics, and much more built in, so by finding a good CRM solution, you'll be covering a lot of the areas I mentioned above. You'll want to start with a CRM tool and then supplement that based on the inherent functionality that you can leverage, and what isn't going to work for you. Try to use what you have available first before purchasing additional software, then talk to other marketers. Building your tech stack isn't easy, but building it right from the start so that all of the solutions work together versus independently is the key. Remember that as you scale—as you build more solutions, enter more markets, employ more people—your marketing efforts will skyrocket, so keeping things as simple as possible will help prevent marketing from becoming the roadblock in the company's growth.

Metric Definition

As with most things in life, you're not going to be effective without goals and goals need to be measurable, right? You need to be able to clearly articulate your successes and failures and you need to be able to first define how you plan to measure them. You need goals. Figure out early the metrics that you will monitor and share, even if it's only a guess in the beginning. It doesn't matter, but you need a starting point because any metrics you develop can and will change over time. And similar to the situation in martech, there are plenty of metrics to choose from. Some common marketing metrics include leads, marketing qualified leads (MQLs), sales accepted leads (SALs), marketing return on investment (ROI), customer acquisition cost (CAC), or conversion rates. We can't tell you what the best option will be for your business, it's likely a combination of several of these, but establish your metrics early and measure them often, and over time.

Being able to report on trends will be one of the most valuable aspects of your marketing operations, and you'll need ample time for good trend analysis. At Return Path, we developed a sophisticated marketing operations function that was the cornerstone of our marketing department. We had real-time dashboards, weekly scorecards, bi-weekly pipeline meetings, and many other forms of monthly, quarterly, and annual reporting. It helped us plan for the year, showcase our results, adjust our tactics, and celebrate our successes.

While gathering all this data can be cumbersome and time-consuming, it's worth it because all the data on trends, all the data from pipeline, and all other data we collect not only provide benchmarks but also feed into our strategic plan. Yes, it takes time to develop, but once you start and have some runway, these metrics help determine both short- and long-term goals.

6

Supporting the Company Culture

After your brand has been built and a demand generation strategy has been established, you can turn some of your attention inward. There's a significant role for a CMO and the marketing organization as a whole to play in nurturing the company culture and positioning the company as not only a great one to work *with* but a great one to work *for*.

From recruitment marketing efforts, to facilitating internal communications, to supporting employee engagement, there are countless opportunities for Marketing to collaborate with the HR/People/Talent team and lend marketing support to either spearhead or provide resources for employee-targeted initiatives. Very early in your startup you should work to develop a collaborative, proactive relationship with the People team. Don't wait for them to reach out to you for marketing ideas that can augment your culture, but set up a regular cadence with them to discuss and plan how Marketing can add to the culture.

Recruitment Marketing

As your startup grows and evolves, attracting the right talent will be a major focus of the Chief People Officer and the People team. Lucky for them, there is a lot of support Marketing can provide when it comes to positioning the company as an attractive work environment.

The first step is to develop a clear value proposition for potential employees. The People team can provide all the information you need about benefits, values, and the employee experience and Marketing can apply their expertise to craft a compelling story to drive home what makes your company an exceptional place to work. That story and the defined value proposition will be the cornerstone of your recruitment marketing efforts.

Next, it's important to partner with the People team to establish a presence in places where candidates evaluate potential employers, such as Glassdoor. The same way Marketing maintains an active presence on social media sites, as the company grows, the People team will be actively monitoring these types of sites in order to provide insight into the company culture and respond to any feedback. Working with the People team to create appropriate messaging, design custom images, and build the required content for the site will help to ensure that the company is putting its best foot forward and delivering a consistent message to prospective employees.

It's no secret that your website is your greatest asset when it comes to demand generation, and it also has a major role to play when it comes to educating prospective employees about your company and culture. Creating a Career page that is easily accessible from your website allows you to share all the things that make your company great—like your core values and work benefits—and also provides a channel to promote open positions and links to online applications.

Finally, Marketing can provide significant support to the People team in producing materials and swag to use in recruitment events. Just as brand consistency is important when it comes to building awareness and driving demand for new business, it is equally important when it comes to attracting and converting job candidates. Work with the People team to think creatively about how to stand out in potentially crowded markets and provide insight that will inform and engage the talent you're looking to hire. From unique swag, to digital sessions, to email campaigns, there are all kinds of ways you can collaborate to develop innovative approaches.

At Lev, a marketing-focused consultancy where Holly worked, the marketing and talent teams are closely aligned in recruitment efforts, especially in developing the Career section of our website. As with many companies, the Careers page is one of the most highly trafficked pages, and it's important to provide useful insights to inform and attract talent while also making it easy for those candidates to apply. The Marketing team relied on the Talent team to identify the key pieces of information they knew would attract talent and address common questions, while the talent team relied on Marketing to build a website experience to clearly convey that information and integrate with their hiring platform.

We've also collaborated to find ways to communicate with and engage our talent pool, especially those who may be a good fit at Lev but who don't align to an opening at that specific point in time. Marketing and the talent team collaborated to capture information from candidates interested in specific opportunities, communicated important updates via marketing automation to them, and hosted recruitment-focused webinars. The webinars in particular allow the talent team to provide an overview of Lev—our culture, benefits, and primary roles—to large groups of potential candidates while utilizing the skills and technology available to the Marketing team to execute the event, including promotion, registration, webinar hosting, and post-webinar follow-up.

Internal Communications

As a startup, you may be a "one-room" company at first and internal communications might be less of a priority. After all, with a dozen people sharing an office, it's easy to communicate, but as you grow, add locations, or work remotely, internal communications become more of a priority. Taking internal communications seriously and professionally from the outset will set you up for future success.

As marketers, we understand the value of sharing a message multiple times over various channels in order to make an impression on our target audience. Don't they say that a person needs to hear a message seven times before it sinks in? That approach is no different when it comes to communicating internally, and even then people might not get your message!

People register and retain information in a wide variety of ways. Some prefer in-person communication, some prefer email, some prefer Slack or Teams messages, and some people only look up at a poster in the kitchen. There's no right answer and no singular approach that will satisfy everyone's needs. This makes communicating one message across multiple channels a necessity, and an area where Marketing can make an impact.

In alignment with the People team, the CMO and marketing team can play a big role in advocating for employees as a key audience and strategically approaching internal communications in ways that will maximize engagement. From working with the CEO and other fellow executives on company-wide meetings to facilitating the sending of company-wide emails, Marketing can provide oversight in ensuring that we're communicating clearly and effectively with employees, no matter the message.

Employee Engagement

Everyone on the executive team has a role to play when it comes to growing and nurturing the company's culture and delivering a positive employee experience. For the CMO, however, the opportunities are particularly fun.

In the push to launch a product, feature, or offering, the emphasis is rightfully on getting the job done and checking all the boxes when it comes to external promotion. It can be easy, however, to overlook educating everyone internally about the work being done and celebrating the wins collectively. Building an internal launch plan into the overall marketing execution for a launch ensures that this piece of the puzzle doesn't get overlooked, and provides an opportunity for the company as a whole to be on the same page and take a moment to celebrate the achievement.

Marketing also has a role to play in supporting internal events. While we wouldn't advocate for Marketing taking full ownership of organizing employee events like employee appreciation activities or holiday gatherings—that is more appropriately the purview of the People team—there is value Marketing can add in providing creative ideas, producing swag, and supporting logistics planning.

Lastly, as the company transitions from startup to scaleup, your employee population will rise and bring with it the opportunity to partner with the People team in introducing affinity groups. From facilitating the sending of internal communications to designing text treatments or other design assets for the groups, to providing marketing expertise to help these affinity groups grow and expand their impact across the organization, there is a lot Marketing can do to add value to these groups and support them in their missions.

7

Breaking Down Marketing's Functions

The three primary foundations of marketing—brand, sales, and culture—are not standalone, esoteric ideas but are actually supported by seven primary functions: Brand, Digital, Events, Content and Communications, Product Marketing, Operations, and Sales Development. Depending on the needs of the business and the size of the marketing organization, how you execute against these functions and organize your team may be wildly different. For a startup, one individual may cover multiple or all of these responsibilities, while a scaleup may have teams of contributors supporting each function.

No matter the size of your marketing team or the business itself, no matter whether you're a B2B, B2C, or nonprofit, no matter whether you have no budget or an unlimited budget, it is essential to understand the value each function brings to the overall marketing strategy and the ways in which they can intersect in order to get more out of each campaign and deliver maximum impact.

Brand

As we've discussed already, building and maintaining the company brand are the primary responsibility of Marketing. Your brand is not only the visual elements—the logo, color pallet, and supporting design elements—it's also the textual elements—the tone and personality you want to convey and the core messaging behind those elements. The combination of these is the driving force behind everything Marketing creates. It's not uncommon for people to think of the brand as one or two things, like the website, the logo, and the tagline and it's your job to continually remind people that the brand is more than that. The brand embodies your company values, culture, personality, go-to-market strategy, products, services, and more. Your brand will set you apart from competitors, it will attract customers to you, and it will help potential employees reach out to you. The brand is definitely more than a website and a logo!

We developed a deep appreciation for the power of a brand at Return Path and regardless of our role—whether an individual contributor or a manager—we considered ourselves to be the lead brand ambassadors throughout our time with the company. We adopted a simple mission: if anything had a Return Path logo on it, we were responsible for it. That means apparel, websites, event banners, invitations—anything with our logo was something that we were responsible for. With that directive, ensuring the consistent application of our brand standards became our primary goal.

Ideally, your brand should provide you, the marketing team, vendors, and employees "freedom within a framework." Simply put, what that means is brand guidelines are supposed to provide a framework for the rest of the organization to operate within. The brand provides the basics—the colors, icons, language, logo, templates, etc.—and then enables the rest of the company to leverage those assets in order to deliver on their own objectives. They are empowered to take the framework the brand provides and mold it into their use case.

If you don't create "freedom within a framework," you'll constantly be battling the fast-moving renegades within your company, the people who believe that getting their content out into the market, or into the hands of customers quickly, is the critical task. They don't think about whether or not their content follows the brand guidelines or is consistent with other collateral. And, honestly, they have a reasonable point of view. But if you don't have a framework, you will spend your time both policing infractions of your brand and a lot of time recreating what's been done to fit it into your brand. Marketing will become the obstacle within the organization instead of the enabler, and Marketing will be blamed for all sorts of things in the market. Take it from us, the best thing you can do as a startup CMO is to create brand guidelines for the rest of the company, provide clear, repeatable training, and set them up for success for others to use them as they see fit.

It's important to note that consistency is key when it comes to your brand. Brand guidelines, or that framework to work within, ensure that throughout the customer lifecycle, the company is delivering a consistent, repeatable, and recognizable experience for your audience. The most-recognized brands have this consistency, and it not only outlasts the customer experience, but they are unique so you would never confuse Apple with McDonald's, for example. A random person should be able to look at any output of your company—a page on the website, a presentation from an account executive, an invoice from Finance, or a help article from Customer Service—and immediately recognize it as belonging to your brand. This not only drives brand awareness, it also builds trust. And that trust is essential when it comes to identifying, winning, and growing your customer base.

That consistency should be evident not only in the visual style of your output, but in the voice as well. Tone, word choice, cadence; all those play a significant role in communicating a brand. Is your brand friendly and off-beat or is it more straightforward and buttoned-up? What is the tone of voice your audience will respond most positively to? Your brand voice should reflect that. Any marketer probably remembers (or is at least aware of) the famous "I'm a Mac. I'm a PC." commercials of the late 2000s. They're an excellent study in how brand voice and visuals can come together to communicate the desired message. You can even look at commercials for fast food chains like McDonald's, Burger King, and Arby's. Not only is their look unique from one another, the way they speak and the words they use are completely different as well, but aligned with each particular brand.

For a CMO, the brand marketing work doesn't stop once the brand has been established and the guidelines have been shared across the organization. Rather, that is just the first step of many. Think about your brand as being as alive as you or me. It's a living and breathing contributor to your company, and should be treated as such. The best brands receive constant attention and fine-tuning to keep pace with the nonstop change and evolution that naturally occurs within any business.

At Return Path, the Brand and Digital Marketing team made it a habit to set aside time each year to evaluate every aspect of our brand, from our color palette to our core messaging. Typically, we took two to three days to focus exclusively on this work, making it clear to the rest of the company that we were "heads down" and purposefully avoiding the interruption of work on other projects. During that time, we would brain-storm, explore changes, make revisions, and fully execute any updates. Particularly when the company moved from three lines of business to one after a couple of divestitures, this time was invaluable in helping us determine how we would visualize and contextualize this shift. From reworking our color palette, redrafting our core messaging, and updating all of our company-wide templates and assets, the shift in the business was reflected and rolled out in our brand guidelines and assets.

No matter the level of output, make it a priority to evaluate your brand and associated assets on an annual basis to ensure they're doing everything you need them to do. The annual evaluation is a minimum—if your situation changes dramatically, if you acquire a company, divest a business unit, enter a new business, expand globally, or any other major event happens, you'll want to rethink your brand more often. You'll want to ask basic questions about your brand, like, are you still communicating your value props effectively? Are there new design trends that help you visually communicate your brand in a more interesting way? Are your brand guidelines working (or not working) once they're in the hands of the sales or service teams? As the CMO, you need to make sure you're creating space for you and your team on a regular basis to evaluate and refine your brand. You'll need to ensure that the brand continues to grow and improve in line with the company as a whole.

A final note on the brand: an individual brand marketer or brand team makes the greatest impact when they act in service of the rest of the company and a lot of times this means doing day-to-day tasks that are not necessarily visionary. You might be tasked with cleaning up PowerPoint presentations or creating another iteration of a one-pager for a specific use case. That isn't glamorous work but in doing that you're helping to put the company's best foot forward in as many instances as possible, and that provides value. As Matt used to say regularly when congratulating our design team, "Thank you for making us look so great to the world." The key for the CMO is to establish the ground rules for engaging those tasked with brand marketing (for example, establishing a project request system), enforcing those rules consistently, and delivering the requested work on time and above expectations. Doing this not only demonstrates the impact using the brand to its fullest can have (I've seen some incredible before and after decks in my time) but also builds relationships and fosters collaboration between Marketing and other functions in the organization. Seeing the marketing team actively make work better, deliver what is needed, and continually push its own boundaries influences how the rest of the company perceives the marketing organization as a whole.

Digital

Once you have a handle on your brand, the next step is translating it to digital marketing. Your digital marketing activities are where you take the combination of your visual brand (the logo, the colors, the design elements) and textual brand (the core messages, the tone of the writing, the personality) and bring them to life. That is where things really start to get fun.

For a startup, digital marketing provides the greatest opportunity for building brand awareness and driving demand for your product or service. Basic digital marketing activities include creating a website, establishing an email marketing program, generating a social media presence, and running digital advertising campaigns. Each of these is powerful on their own, more powerful when combined together, and fully maximized when collaborating with the other marketing functions.

Website

At Return Path, we often said one 100x25 pixel Call To Action (CTA) on our website was our most valuable marketing asset. That 100x25 pixel is about the size of a postage stamp—and it's our most valuable asset? Well, it was our "Request a Demo" button and it was responsible for more than 10% of our lead generation per year and was consistently our highest performer when it came to converting leads to bookings. That's the power of digital (and marketing, really): it's not an end in itself, it's an enabler, an accelerator, it's a sieve that culls the good from the bad, the serious from the inquisitive. Even something as minor as a button on a website can be a powerful tool.

Thinking more broadly than a small CTA, the website itself is the storefront of your company. It will be one of the first introductions a person has to your brand, your offering, and your mission, so it's critical that you have a firm understanding of what you need to communicate and what actions you want visitors to take.

A strict focus on the desired action you want visitors to take should drive every choice you make when it comes to your website's design, content, and layout. At Return Path (as with most good SaaS companies), that Request a Demo button was impactful because we intentionally directed visitors to it through visual cues, like the color of the button and its position on the page, and through limiting other possible actions they could take. For example, on gated landing pages—pages with a form the visitor must complete in order to get to a content piece like a whitepaper, video, or other branded asset—the only options were to A) submit the form, B) return to the home page, or C) click the Request a Demo button.

Your desired action may not always be to get the visitor to request a demo, or to only take one action. At DePauw University, I (Holly) managed alumni communications and one of my first undertakings was to streamline our website content in order to focus alumni action around specific goals—Go, Give, Help, and Connect. Each of those pillars had a specific action we wanted people to take, and all four were critical when it came to engaging our alumni base and keeping them connected to the institution. For each goal, there was one specific "best action" we wanted to drive alumni towards:

- Go = register for an event

- Give = make a donation

- Help = sign up to volunteer

- Connect = create an account in the online directory

By having a clear perspective on the action(s) you want your visitors to take, you can then build a website experience to create the opportunities and deliver the messaging to make that action more likely.

Email

Another foundational element of any digital marketing program is email marketing. We promise you that email is not dead, and won't be anytime soon. In fact, there is a significant amount of research that shows the incredible ROI an email program offers; as much as four times the ROI of other channels. The DMA, for example, reports that in 2021 email returned $43 for every $1 spent.[1] With almost 4 billion daily email users,

---

1. See https://blog.hubspot.com/marketing/email-marketing-stats

the ability to access our email on laptops, mobile devices, and even our watches, and the rise of 5G, access to the inbox has never been easier.

There are a few straightforward things you can do to ensure that your email marketing program is successful in engaging your audience:

- **Deliver meaningful content.** First and foremost, you need to be sending emails with content your audience will care about. Whether it's information about a product launch or your latest content release, make sure you understand the value it provides to the subscriber and describe it clearly and concisely.

- **Have a clear call to action.** When you overload an email with links and buttons, or forget to include one at all, you make it hard for the reader to know what to do. It can be tough, but try to limit your emails to one specific call to action. If you do have more than one CTA (in a newsletter, for example), lead with the action you most want the reader to take.

- **Know and follow regulations.** Regulations that govern privacy, like GDPR and CCPA, are strict and complex. Make sure you both understand how the rules apply to you and build up an email program that fits within the guideline. It will always be tempting to try and go around the rules, like sending an email to a group who isn't opted in, but it's rarely worth the potential risk and usually doesn't return worthwhile engagement.

- **Make testing part of your process.** Consumer interests change as often as the seasons. Make sure you're consistently testing the various aspects of your emails to see what's working. From the subject line, to the button color, to the tone of voice, to the entire design, testing your options to see what works best will only make your emails more impactful.

- **Get creative with growing your list.** Growing your subscriber list should always be top of mind, and there's a lot of ways you can go about gaining opted-in readers. Tactics like email signature banners, one-to-one outreach to current customers, callouts on your website or blog, are a solid start. You can also make it more of an experience, like building the opt-in process into your onboarding campaign or incentivizing subscribers to get their friends to sign up.

Social

Social strategy can be a bit of a wild card. There's no debate that having a presence across various platforms is table stakes, but the ROI can be wildly different based on industry and target audience. Whether social engagement is driving sales or not, being active on social media will give you valuable consumer insight, and taking as much time to engage in social listening as you do in social posting will help you stay on top of trends, changing attitudes, and general sentiment.

At the most simplistic level, there are three things you should have a plan for in order to be successful in your approach to social media.

1. **Plan for being active.** Whether it's Facebook, X, Instagram, LinkedIn or something else, you get what you give. Posting your own content and updates is important, but it's equally if not more important to engage with other profiles too. Whether they're customers, partners, or complementary brands, sharing, liking, and commenting can go a long way in building relationships with other individuals and companies that can broaden your reach.

2. **Plan your rules of engagement.** Trolls are a part of the game when it comes to social media. Whether it's an aggressive competitor, a disgruntled former customer or employee, or someone just looking to cause trouble, negativity will find its way into your feed. Our advice: never delete negative comments and remember you're not obligated to respond. There may come a time when the record needs to be corrected, but more often than not it's better to simply let the mean, false, or provocative comments go.

3. **Plan to make others aware.** At some point, you will engage with a current or future customer, and it will be important that you have a plan for how to make others aware of those interactions. Did a customer post something good or bad? Let their account rep know. Is there an issue? Know who you need to alert in IT, Engineering, or Customer Service. Understanding who needs to know when you stumble across potentially useful information will go a long way in making your social presence valuable.

At the end of the day, know what it is you can realistically get out of your social strategy. For B2B brands, sometimes just being present is enough and realistically it may never be a major lead driver. That's OK, but being there is still important and builds trust, legitimacy, and brand awareness. For B2C brands, social can play a much larger role. Don't get too caught up in trying to be what you're not, or trying to go viral. Represent your brand consistently and accurately above all else. Establishing that consistency and demonstrating your engagement with your customers (and future customers) can go a long way in building loyalty.

Advertising

The internet is a noisy, crowded place. Luckily, digital advertising provides an opportunity for marketers to make sure their brand stands out. From pay-per-click (PPC), to display, to search, to social, there is a lot of potential for promoting your product or services and reaching your target audience.

Digital advertising can be complex, especially when it comes to managing your budget, but there are a few basic concepts you can keep in mind to ensure that you're using those dollars effectively while your campaigns are running.

- **Be concise.** Almost every digital advertising option comes with a character limit. Know what it is and stick to it. If nothing else, writing for ads is a great way to tighten up all of your messaging because it has the most specific constraints. When you can make your case for engagement in as few words as possible, you're onto something good.

- **Have a clear call to action.** Every ad you're running is going to be driving the user to do something. Do you want them to give up their contact information to download a report? Do you want them to request a demo? Do you want them to register for an event? Know what the desired outcome is, make it clear in the ad, and make it clear on the landing page.

- **Stay on top of conversion.** Forget the seller's mantra, "ABC: always be closing." For marketers, it's "ABO: always be optimizing." Clicks are great, but conversions are what counts. It's important to understand which ads are driving clicks, but if you aren't seeing good conversion on the desired action, have a plan of action to make adjustments. Maybe your copy needs to be clearer, your layout needs to be rearranged, or you need to try an entirely new angle.

- **Try new things.** This is relevant for your messaging and ad design, but also for the types of digital advertising you're using. Maybe you're putting everything you've got into search advertising, but haven't given social advertising a try. Or you're running some successful PPC and display ads, but you've not really experimented with Account Based Marketing yet. Each approach offers its own value, and you won't know the perfect recipe for your success until you try out a few variations.

While we're on the topic, we should dip our toes into the wider pool of advertising possibilities, which of course no book or book section on marketing can ignore. In the world of B2C, digital advertising offers speed and flexibility, but there are many other avenues to take that provide the reach you may need. From billboards, to television, to radio, to newspapers or magazines, there are considerable channels to explore. As with any promotional activity, the most important thing to consider is whether the delivery method enables you to deliver your message in the most impactful, effective way possible. In the world of startups, traditional offline advertising is a rarity both due to its lack of addressability (although that is improving for most channels) and due to its sheer expense. Although we see the occasional proverbial Super Bowl dot-com ad, and a handful of billboards driving on the 101 between San Francisco and Silicon Valley, those don't represent enough of a startup CMO's advertising endeavors to warrant a lot of discussion here. If you find yourself being pulled into traditional advertising channels because your business is taking off explosively and you're a strong Direct to Consumer brand, you're likely beyond being in the startup phase and have much larger budgets and agency support to lean on!

Omni-Channel

One way to maximize the impact of your digital marketing efforts is to deliver the same message across as many channels as possible. What's important, though, is how you craft those messages to fit within the specific channel. As Marshall McLuhan said, "the medium is the message" and nowhere is this more practically applicable than in digital marketing today. Although McLuhan first wrote this concept down in 1964 in the advent of television, his concept is given more weight by the abundance of "mediums"—or communication channels—we have today. Think of it this way: if you were going to share one thought across all of your social channels, the output would be very different between Facebook, X, Instagram, and LinkedIn. That's because each medium dictates the way messages are best delivered: X favors short and sweet, Instagram is all about the visuals, Facebook is best suited for longer, more personal content, and LinkedIn is the home of concise, professional posts. Now apply that to the entirety of your digital marketing program, not just social channels.

If you can take one message and tell it on your website, through an email campaign, across your preferred social channels, and in digital ads, you're well on your way to an omni-channel marketing campaign and you've greatly maximized the output of that single message. Duplicated across a variety of value propositions, product offerings, or brand-building messages, you have a backlog of campaigns you can run to build up your output and get your content into the market.

The beautiful thing about digital marketing is that you have the capacity to continually make changes to optimize against your goals. Unlike approaches like print marketing, for example, where the message is locked in once it's out in the world, digital channels give marketers the opportunity to test, pivot, rewrite, and reimagine constantly. For a startup, this level of flexibility is a huge advantage, especially as you work to find your voice, build your brand, and establish the narrative that will help your company grow.

The Case for Grouping Brand and Digital Together

We are passionate supporters of the notion that brand and digital marketing go hand-in-hand in companies where the overwhelming majority of advertising efforts are digital (if, as we noted above, your brand has achieved some level of escape velocity and is pursuing a lot of offline advertising, then the previous sentence does not hold!). You can't have a strong digital marketing presence if you don't have a solid understanding of your brand. Your brand informs every digital move you make—how you speak, what content you create, and how everything fits together. Similarly, you can't have a strong brand without taking advantage of the opportunity digital marketing provides to constantly test, iterate, and refine your brand across a variety of channels. Your digital marketing efforts inform your brand evolution—how to strengthen the brand, how you adapt to new trends and technologies, and how you tell your story in new ways. Like we said, brand and digital go hand-in-hand.

Having both a brand and digital team is a luxury, most likely only attainable for a company more in scaleup mode, but thinking about the two functions together is absolutely achievable for a startup with limited marketing resources. At Lev, Holly was lucky enough to have one team member who was a powerhouse when it came to both brand and digital marketing. Having both design and digital execution within one role has allowed us to move quickly in building our brand and our digital efforts simultaneously. As we build the website, we're refining our messaging; as we elevate our brand design, we're redesigning the website; as we test new channels, like digital advertising, we're finding new ways to tell the Lev story.

While a full-fledged brand and digital team may be a longer-term goal, the startup CMO can still make it a priority to find one or two people who can execute brand and digital marketing initiatives together to ensure that the constant growth and innovation that need to happen are adequately supported.

8

Events

Nick started his marketing career in events and it's a marketing channel that we're particularly passionate about. We know "events" sounds old-school and traditional, especially after talking about technology and digital, but remember—marketing involves promoting, selling, and distributing products and services in ways that build the brand, generate leads, and solidify the company culture. Events are unique in that they promote all three of those objectives. If you do it well, event marketing can be the single most effective approach for achieving marketing goals. If you don't do it well, however, it can quickly eat away at your budget and time. It can tarnish your brand, reduce leads, and actually hurt your culture. Besides that, if you don't do event marketing well, you'll waste a good amount of productivity. Contrary to how most people view event marketing, the "event" isn't the most important thing to concentrate on. Effective event marketing requires equal investment in pre-event activity, event execution, and post-event follow-up. So, the event is the middle of a three-stage marketing model, and not the single most important thing.

We should note that COVID-19 created an interesting twist in events. Not being able to physically gather and having to cancel all marketing events is leaving a huge gap in many Marketing team's demand generation plans. At the same time that COVID-19 has impacted events, it has also spurred new innovative and creative approaches on how to pull off incredible virtual experiences. Webinars and virtual events are now the norm, and since individuals are stuck working at home, many are still hungry for these types of experiences. It's interesting to see how the pandemic has challenged marketers to think differently. Some of the innovations include sending a package a day prior to the event, including the itinerary, some swag (a tee shirt, some gifts), and even some food to keep people satisfied for that block of time. We expect events to continue to evolve and to push the limits.

Before getting into event planning, you need to know the "why" behind your event strategy. What is it you want to accomplish? Are you looking for net new leads or to nurture leads? Do you see event marketing as a way to advance existing opportunities or to retain and upsell clients? Or perhaps you want to generate awareness around a new product. Maybe it's a combination of more than one of these. Regardless, you'll need to know the "why" behind your event because this will allow you to choose the right event, set and measure the right goals, and put together the best overall strategy. Once you know the "why," you can then determine what event or combination of events will best achieve what your business needs.

Types of Events

Generally, events fall into one of two categories: third-party or self-hosted. Third-party events include trade shows, conferences, and partner events. They are hosted by a third-party and for the most part you are leveraging their audience. Sure, there are ways you can target and engage a segment of the audience, but you are largely paying a premium to be part of something that is already established. In third-party events you should expect to pay a sponsorship fee and receive in return various entitlements based on your investment. Third-party events can be great for getting access to an audience that you otherwise would not have access to. I said "can be" because the event itself might not lead to anything unless you do the pre-event planning and the post-event follow-up.

Self-hosted events are the events that you host and where you are responsible for ensuring you get the target audience to participate. You'll have more control over most aspects of self-hosted events, but also more responsibility. Self-hosted events can take just about any form you can think of, ranging from networking events, to hospitality events, educational events, webinars, customer events, user conferences, client advisory boards, and more.

Event Planning

Once you know the "why," or what you are looking to accomplish, you're ready to start your selection process and plan out your event strategy. Event planning is not a one-time task but more likely a series of tasks that should be planned out over a period of time. If your company is new to event marketing, you may want to carefully select one or two events to experiment with before building a more comprehensive plan. One of the best things you can do, even as an early-stage startup, is to map out your event calendar a year in advance. Sure, things will change. But as long as you allow for some flexibility, mapping out your event calendar a year in advance is a healthy exercise for several reasons.

First, mapping it out will allow you to build your event strategy in conjunction with other marketing and company initiatives. Things like product launches, major content releases, quarter end, other marketing campaigns, and internal events can be taken into consideration. There's nothing more ineffective than doing a marketing campaign weeks before or after a well-attended event. The right event in combination with a product launch can be a great way to boost excitement around the launch and also provides your event with fresh content.

Second, by mapping your event calendar, you'll be able to integrate your event strategy with seasonality. In a lot of businesses, the beginning of the year, end of the year, and midsummer are not optimal times for events, for obvious reasons. So, look to avoid those times and instead spread out events throughout the year to reduce strain for the teams who work on and leverage events.

Third, planning out a year ahead will really help with your demand generation planning. At Return Path, historical data gave us a pretty decent idea of the types of business results we could expect from most events. By itself, that data was just an interesting "good to know," but being able to map those events out along with other marketing initiatives provided us with a demand generation heat map. Now we had something powerful. We could see when we were light or heavy during certain periods and we could easily adjust our event schedule or other initiatives accordingly.

Partnering with Sales

No team in your company will be more interested in what marketing is doing with events than Sales. The relationship between Sales and Marketing is always an important one and it will become magnified during events. The sales team plays a crucial part in staffing and speaking at events. They'll also have ideas on products or services to feature and they'll want to contribute to the invite list and experience. Collaborating successfully with Sales can have a heavy influence on the level of success for an event. You'll want to work with Sales Leadership to know what types of events are needed, what goals they would like to achieve, and gather any ideas about event location. A thoughtful conversation with Sales Leadership will cover topics like quotas, existing pipeline, opportunities in flight, partnerships, staffing needs, geography, and bandwidth. These conversations happen during the event planning stage, not a few days before or after the event, and they inform your overall event strategy.

Another way to collaborate with Sales is to look for opportunities where you can leverage location and people. We were always big advocates on maximizing team travel time in-market when we're doing our event planning. So, if we were planning to travel to NYC in March for an event, we'd figure out what prospect or client meetings could be arranged in conjunction with that travel. Could we create a unique experience for a specific prospect or client by leveraging the event? Could we create a separate experience the day before or after an event and leverage a company thought leader or executive who will also be in attendance? Thinking carefully during the planning stages about the event, the people, the location, and what you want to accomplish will allow you to create pre- and post-mini-events that are more intimate and can build relationships with clients and potential clients.

Pre-Event

We referenced earlier that effective event marketing isn't only about the event itself. The work done before, during, and after are equally important. It's easy to lose sight of the fact that the pre- and post-event activities are equally important because for most people in your company and for event participants, the event itself will have a specific date, venue, and marketing message, so it's natural for them to think that the event is THE EVENT. It's best to constantly remind others that event marketing has pre- and post-activities that help to make an event a revenue generator. For third-party events, it's likely you'll get a pre-event attendee list and you should leverage this as soon as possible, although sometimes you may not get it until right before the event. Your goal when you receive the attendee list is to build unique experiences only available at the event, and comb through the attendee list to identify who in your target audience would benefit from these unique experiences. Ask your Sales or Sales Development team to reach out personally to the right individuals to engage with these attendees in advance. For example, at Return Path one unique experience we offered was complimentary on-site consultation. Marketing would create an email template explaining the value, often including the normal dollar value of this now complementary consultation, and we'd ask the individual to reserve their time. The event team arranged a schedule, space, and staffing plan for these meetings to happen. We would be offering a unique opportunity for attendees to engage with us and nine times out of ten the attending individual would walk away with real value from the time spent with us.

After the complimentary consultation, it made it a whole lot easier to continue discussing ways to work together. You should also share the attendee list with the internal team members attending the event in person so that they can arrange in-person meetings. And for any account owner, whether attending in person or not, we always made sure they knew who from their account base would be attending the event, and we provided account owners multiple ways to engage with their base. They could engage through one of our complimentary consultations, attend our speaking session, stop by our booth to pick up something special, invite them to a VIP experience available to us as sponsors, or invite them to one of our own dinners or ancillary events we were planning in conjunction with the main event. The point is, you'll have an attendee list but it's not enough to know who's there so you can say hello, but to know who's there so you can engage with them in ways that lead to a deeper connection.

For self-hosted events, it's all about getting the right people to the event in the first place. Without the right people in attendance, you're wasting time, money, and effort. Marketing can promote an event to targeted lists through marketing emails (honoring individual preferences, of course), social, website, and other channels. However, the real value in an event happens through personalization. Sales and Sales Development typically know the value of events, and most of the time they will be chomping at the bit for the opportunity to engage. Regardless of the enthusiasm of Sales and Sales Development, Marketing still needs to fully participate and do whatever possible to help make the event a success. Provide a list of potential customers for Sales to target, provide templates with the marketing message you want, and have them reach out themselves to prospects. Don't forget that Marketing can engage with customers and prospects personally as well. Our field marketers got pretty good at building relationships with individuals in our industry and were a great channel for us to get the right people to attend our own events.

Event Execution

For event execution itself, we'd focus on two main elements. First, make sure that you provide an amazing attendee experience. Regardless of the type of event—virtual, in-person, conference, seminar, networking—think through every aspect of the attendee experience. How is your brand physically represented? Who or what is their first engagement point at the event? Is the content valuable? Is the time and place right? And, ultimately, is it a memorable experience? The second element is to be present. It sounds obvious, but how many times have you gone to an event and seen the hosts engaging with each other, and not with the attendees? Ensure that all team members attending the event, regardless of level or function, are representing the company at all times and engaging whenever possible with attendees. They should be fully present and that means talking to attendees, participating and engaging in content, being a thoughtful host, and contributing to the event. Teamwork at events is invaluable for a good attendee experience, and it's a good way to build on your company culture.

Post-Event

The final phase of event marketing is the post-event. This is where some of the most important work begins. As soon as possible, you should get your attendee data to your CRM so you can measure results. Follow up with event attendees as soon as possible, which can be as simple as saying thank you or sorry we missed you. Provide content or takeaways for those who attended as well as those who did not attend. Establish next steps. Make sure Sales Development and Sales teams know the details of the event for effective personal follow-up. Find a way to document and share notes from conversations that happened at the event. Keep the momentum from the event going. How do you keep that momentum? Share the good, the bad, and the ugly from the event. Share what went well and what you would change, share the "wins," and share the lessons learned. Events are not standalone and discrete but are things that will be repeated in the future and even if they're not repeated, the lessons learned will transfer to your next event. If you can capture people's ideas and thoughts about the event while it's still fresh, you'll be ahead of the game for your next event.

Using Data

Events are big investments for every company, regardless of stage of growth because they are a high investment in cash, time, and staff. Figuring out where and when to invest should be deeply rooted in business results and historical data. You'll need to measure the right things, over time and consistently, in order to have this data in the first place but common metrics like leads, MQLs, opportunities, pipeline, sourced bookings, influence, and ROI should definitely be tracked.

We found that starting with leads and then monitoring conversion to pipeline and to closed-won business were the most valuable indicators of event value, with sourced bookings winning overall. You can take this sourced number divided by the investment amount to provide ROI, which is equally important. I found influence was more valuable as a metric for impact on our customer base, which we measured separately. One additional reason to support reporting on event impact consistently over time is the fact that, depending on your sales cycle, you may not be able to see value from an event for some time. It could take one quarter, two quarters, maybe even a year or longer. Be patient, and don't get frustrated if you don't see ROI quickly. There are plenty of ways to nurture and move along event lists and conversations.

9

Content and Communications

Content comes in many different shapes and sizes. From slide decks, to one-pagers, to customer stories, to blog posts, to podcast episodes, to webinars, to infographics, to press releases, to white papers, to ebooks ... the list goes on and on. No matter the final output, though, the objective from a marketing perspective is always the same: to add value. Each bit of content, no matter how big or small, needs to have value for prospects, value for customers, and value for the business. Without that value, you're just wasting everyone's time.

So how does a content marketing strategy add value to your company? It actually checks all three boxes of your marketing goals: (1) it helps build your brand; (2) it drives demand for sales; and (3) it supports the company culture. Three out of three!

- **Brand building.** Producing and promoting content that addresses your target audience and provides insight into challenges you know they face reinforce the value your brand can add. By using content to demonstrate that you understand your prospects and customers' needs, and can directly improve their lives for the better—either through your offering or related insight—you build brand awareness and make your offering more relevant to customers, which in turn creates respect, and loyalty.

- **Driving demand.** Your content also serves as a major vehicle for driving demand. On the one hand, Marketing can use content to attract potential customers to engage with your brand and eventually lead them down the path of engaging with your sales team and committing to a purchase. On the other hand, Sales can actively utilize content to engage prospects they are attempting to engage or are already in conversation with. Content that helps to advance their conversations goes a long way in strengthening those relationships and moving prospects closer toward a decision.

- **Company culture.** The content creation process provides an opportunity to engage experts across the organization. By engaging people in all parts of the business, you'll be able to develop a greater diversity of topics and share a broader set of perspectives than if you just feature the same handful of people or departments. It also builds internal affinity to the marketing team, developing stronger relationships between Marketing and other parts of the organization by giving a platform for experts in the company to share their knowledge and fostering cross-collaboration. There are many people in the organization who have ideas and want to share them more broadly, so providing an opportunity for them to do that increases the diversity of ideas and has a greater chance of resonating with people outside your organization.

For any content marketing strategy, it's important to have a clear understanding of the goals you're trying to accomplish with your content. Do you need to demonstrate expertise or address common questions or concerns? Do you need to refine your brand voice or positioning? Having one or even a few specific ideas about the goals you want to accomplish with your content will help focus your efforts and allow you to prioritize ideas and requests.

Once you have those objectives in mind, the next step is to establish realistic expectations about what you can produce. For example, maybe you can commit to one blog post every week, a webinar every month, and a research report every quarter. Setting these goals up front then puts you in a position to outline a content production schedule to work against and communicate that internally in order to get buy-in and (if needed) content development support.

With your goals set and your content calendar roughly established, it's time to start writing. When it comes to content production, it's important to keep a few things in mind. First, everyone will have an opinion, they'll have another way to say something, or they'll have a last-minute change. At the end of the day, the CMO and/or content marketer are responsible for publishing what will serve the best interest of the brand and should be empowered to make the call and publish content when they think it's ready for prime time. That leads into the second point: sometimes done is better than perfect. Very few marketers are sitting on their hands waiting for something new to work on. Instead, they're often overloaded with tasks and moving quickly from one project to the next. With big goals and high expectations, obsessing over the nitpicks or minor changes that prevent a piece of content from going out the door won't help you achieve your goals. Plus, if your content is being distributed digitally, you have the greatest benefit of digital marketing at your disposal: you can make changes at any time!

Public Relations

While blogs, webinars, and ebooks are often top of the list when it comes to content creation, public relations (PR) also falls into the content realm. PR is a misunderstood and rapidly changing arrow in the marketing quiver. Years ago, traditional PR was about writing press releases and working—either directly or via a PR firm—the key journalists who covered your industry. As the media business and reporting in general have changed, PR still includes press releases but is much more often tied to a broader content program with multiple formats of content and multiple channels of distribution. But simply put, if advertising is the art of telling the world your story (via multiple channels), PR is the art of getting other people to tell that story for you.

There is still nothing better and more cost-effective for your marketing than to have a well-known and well-followed influencer tell their audience that your company, your brand, your product or service, is a must-have. Achieving that kind of third-party mention is almost free (at least relative to ad spend), and it carries a 10–100x multiple of credibility since it's not coming from you or your company directly. Sometimes those mentions can be generated by outbound PR work either from an internal team or from an external agency. That was certainly the case in years past when more traditional journalists were the most important and in some cases sole gatekeepers of publicity in whole industries. Today the effort can be a lot more diffuse, with micro-influencers like bloggers or vloggers providing their own mentions or endorsements, leading to more organic social media activity in the form of likes and retweets, which in turn generates other influencers to take notice, and, well, you get the idea.

A strong PR strategy can go an incredibly long way when it comes to brand building and demand generation. For example, at DePauw University, where Holly worked, PR served goals across almost every department—it highlighted notable alumni achievement, recognition received by the University, awards and accomplishments of the faculty, and important staffing changes, all aimed at attracting future students, recruiting talented professors, and energizing the alumni base.

Matt's experience running Marketing at MovieFone (777-FILM) in the 1990s was such that the company's entire trade customer promise—bringing addressable and measurable media to movie marketing for the first time—was given a massive boost by the presence of a major article in one of the company's key trade publications at the time, *The Hollywood Reporter*, that the MovieFone team nurtured for years and referred to as "the holy grail" article. That article generated an increase in sales for the company, but more important, it made other advertising vehicles, including relatively new but powerful internet giants like Yahoo,

Interactive Corp, AOL, and Microsoft, take notice of MovieFone as a company, which was a significant driver of the company's blockbuster $600m sale to AOL less than a year after that article ran.

Content Creation

The biggest hurdle you might face when it comes to content marketing is making a case for its value and creating space for content development to happen. In the midst of brand building, event planning, sales development, and digital campaigns, carving out time to focus on content marketing will be challenging. A lot of times, content creation is the task on your to-do list that keeps getting pushed to the next day. However, content has the power to benefit your brand in unexpected ways so we'd suggest to keep in mind that "done is better than perfect."

At Lev, despite having a small team (just four people in marketing roles, including myself), having a person fully dedicated to content creation was a huge priority. By ramping up our content creation, we were able to address needs across the business while also building brand awareness within our primary lead source, Salesforce. We put a major focus on creating content that was vertical specific because we wanted to address consistent questions from prospects and partners about our expertise in specific industries. Thanks to our close collaboration with the sales organization, we knew they were running up against these questions a lot, so we were able to quickly identify key verticals to focus on and specific questions to address, and start knocking out blog posts, webinars, infographics, and ebooks to create a library of industry-specific content.

This library addressed the initial need of responding to common questions about our experience, but also provided two additional benefits. First, it created a backlog of content for the Sales team to utilize when engaging with new partners and prospects, preempting questions about our industry experience they might have. Second, the high volume of diverse content across verticals established Lev as a thought leader, building up our brand recognition and solidifying trust within Salesforce, a key business partner.

Gated Versus Ungated?

There are two different schools of thought when it comes to whether or not content should be gated. Gating content is a traditional approach to driving demand: a high-value piece of content, like a white paper, is put behind a form to collect contact information. The visitor trades their contact information for access to the content, opening the door for the sales team to engage with the individual. On the other hand, many companies are moving entirely away from the gated content model, choosing instead to make everything available without any barriers to entry. The benefit here is that because visitors are not being asked to trade their information to access content, they're given control over when to offer up that information through other means. For example, a person might voluntarily fill out a contact form or interact with a chatbot, not because they have to gain access to a white paper, but because they want to provide their information. With ungated content you can have a potentially stronger footing for the sales team when they engage with that prospect.

10

Product Marketing

You can have a strong brand, unique corporate positioning, and innovative digital, content, and event strategies, but if you miss the mark on product marketing, the impact will be felt across marketing and your entire business. Product marketing is all about understanding where you fit in the market, the needs of your target audience, and how best to package and position your offering to generate opportunities. Without these foundational elements, every startup or scaleup company will struggle.

While cross-departmental collaboration plays a role in the majority of Marketing's activities, nowhere is that connectivity across the organization more pronounced than within product marketing. Product marketing is the most important marketing you'll do and it requires input and collaboration from nearly every department in a company. Effective product marketing requires intentional collaboration and engagement between Marketing, Product, Finance, Sales, and Customer Service in order to do the following:

- Deliver product offerings and innovation that meet market needs.

- Create client-facing product collateral to drive interest.

- Enable sales and service teams to sell and support product offerings.

So, the marketing of products touches nearly every part of the company and can be make or break for whether or not your company survives. Matt calls it one of a small number of "glue" functions inside the company because it holds so many things together.

Deliver

Understanding your market and the needs of your target audience is the cornerstone of product marketing. You can't effectively position your product if you don't understand the competitive landscape, if you don't know where you fit within that landscape, if you can't say how you are unique, or if you can't articulate how you solve the common pain points of your target audience. Your understanding of all of these components should be a key driver behind your initial offering and how you expand your product or services over time.

The marketplace can be pretty crowded, and product marketing plays an important role in keeping a pulse on the marketplace. Buyers' needs and interests are rarely static, so keeping up with what is happening around you will give you a leg up in remaining at the cutting edge. Similarly, other startups can enter the scene at any time, along with already established companies broadening their reach into new areas. Tasking a product marketer with staying up to speed on the competitive landscape allows both the Marketing and Sales organizations to maintain awareness of what is happening around them and be prepared when entering competitive situations.

Beyond marketing research and competitive intelligence, product marketing also plays an important role in shaping what is delivered to meet the needs of the market. Once you understand your audience, the needs you're addressing, and who you might be up against, using that knowledge to hone in on the right pricing and packing to address those needs within the scope of what is realistic for the targeted buyer is key. Product marketing can ensure that you are taking a competitive offering to the market, with either comparable or (ideally) superior offerings and competitive pricing in order to win business.

Create

Another important role that product marketing fills is the actual creation of assets that support the promotion of your service or offering. Product marketing should lead the charge when it comes to the messaging and positioning associated with your product. This messaging should be different from the messaging and positioning of the company overall, which established the foundation of all of your marketing collateral. Rather than competing with or replacing the corporate messaging, product messaging and positioning should build upon the foundation and provide specificity to dive deeper into the "what" and "how" of the product or solution you're providing.

That messaging then leads to the development of external promotional assets. These could include data sheets, PowerPoint slides, website content, event and webinar content, and demos. Each of these outputs provides a different way to build upon and articulate the product messaging. For example, PowerPoint slides and data sheets are ideal for highlighting value propositions, differentiation within the market, and pricing information. Webinars and demos are perfect for showing off how the product works and showing use cases potential buyers might encounter.

As these assets are developed and executed, you're then set up to launch promotional campaigns to get the assets into the hands of your target audience. From email campaigns to digital advertising to one-to-one outreach from sales development representatives, leveraging your resources across digital, content, and sales development functions will maximize the reach of your assets, rather than simply leaving them in the hands of the sales team for use.

Analyst Relations

Speaking of resources, leveraging industry analysts can really help boost your performance in the market, especially for B2B vendors. You're likely familiar with Gartner, Forrester, and some of the other large firms of the analyst world. Analysts focus on a relatively narrow segment of technology or industry, and they understand these segments better than anyone else. Many businesses rely on industry analysts to keep them informed of industry trends and to inform their buying decisions. Establishing relationships with industry analysts provides weight and feedback to your messaging and product development, and can help influence customer decision making. They also publish research on their segment that can have a real impact on your button line (we rode the Forrester Wave for years at ExactTarget). There are paid and unpaid ways to engage with industry analysts. Naturally, paying customers will get more attention. Regardless, it's worth considering, depending on your category, stage, and budget.

Enable

The last product marketing responsibility to address is the need for centralized enablement of the sales and service teams. Internal enablement can easily become an afterthought, especially in the rush to build a product, set the pricing, build the collateral, and activate the sales engine, but ensuring that time is taken to get the sales and service teams fully up to speed on the product or new offering is a huge component of product marketing.

For sales reps, in order to be successful in selling, they need to know a lot, including:

- What the product or offering is;

- What problem it is solving for the buyer;

- What pricing and packaging offerings are available;

- What discounts they're able to provide;

- What questions or concerns they need to anticipate.

If product marketing can provide clear and concise information to address each of these questions, along with the created promotional assets like data sheets, presentation slides, and demos, the sales team will be in a much stronger position to successfully sell. Without this critical enablement, the message being delivered could be inconsistent, incomplete, or, worst of all, inaccurate.

Similar to the need to enable the sales team, it is also important for product marketing to enable the services team. While they need to know all the same information as the sales team—especially for those in a position to cross-sell or upsell existing customers—they could also need technical training when it comes to troubleshooting or resolving issues related to the product or offering. Training requires close collaboration between Marketing and Product so that the right information and training are delivered to the services team prior to its rollout. Without comprehensive training the services organization is ill-prepared to address customer needs, questions, and concerns.

11

Marketing Operations

Marketing is maturing and has become more complex over the years. The evolving marketing technology landscape, access to more data and channels, and increased value of reporting and marketing ROI have led to the creation of marketing operations as a role within marketing. This development, while subtle, is increasingly common for companies of all sizes and industries. For many companies, marketing operations are the backbone of the marketing organization and that individual or team enables Marketing to increase efficiency and drive results for the team, and ultimately, the full organization. It builds the foundation for your marketing strategy through metrics, process, technology, budgeting, and reporting. Individuals in marketing operations require different skills than a traditional marketer. They are still strategic and creative, but they also need to be analytical and technical, with solid project management experience. Because operations is deeply ingrained across all of marketing, we've touched on several elements already in this chapter. For this section, we'd like to explore four pillars of marketing operations: (1) technology; (2) process; (3) measurement; and (4) strategic planning.

Technology

We discussed the evolving and vast marketing technology landscape. Marketing Operations is responsible for managing the marketing team technology stack. What tools should be used and when is the right time to introduce them? Marketing operations manages the vendor relationships, selection process, implementation, and training. They keep track of the different technologies within marketing, and cross-departmentally, to look for opportunities to integrate or to eliminate redundancy. Because they also help manage the marketing budget, they will have a good idea of when technology spend is becoming disproportionate to overall marketing investment, and when adjustments need to be made.

Process

Efficient process management is always key to scaling and growing, and operations will own and streamline processes on behalf of the marketing organization. At a minimum, you can make a big impact managing processes around budgeting, invoicing, marketing automation, campaigns, and planning. With consistent processes in place and with either an individual or team maintaining a system for everyone to follow, you will be more effective and efficient.

Measurement

Establishing and tracking the key performance indicators for individual campaigns, as well as all of marketing investment, are some of the most important aspects of the marketing operation role. This role needs to ensure that there is alignment across the department on which metrics are tracked, the process for doing so, and sharing out and reporting of those metrics. The marketing operations role also will create and maintain dashboards, scorecards, decks, and reports. Good marketing operations teams not only report on metrics, but have a keen eye for interpreting the data and making recommendations for improvement.

Strategic Planning

Due to a deep understanding of technology, process, and measurement, marketing operations is in the perfect position to be key in the strategic planning for a marketing department. Marketing ops understands lead flow, conversion trends and they have deep visibility of historical campaign performance. Not only can they help manage the monthly, quarterly, and annual planning process, they can make valuable recommendations rooted in data to improve the success and efficiency of your marketing plan.

When to Start Marketing Operations

We've referred to Marketing Operations as a team, but it will likely start out as an individual, such as a marketing operations manager or a director of marketing operations. So, when do you know when this role is needed? For startups, your marketing leader will perform most of the marketing operations duties. However, scaling companies that are starting to see complexity in their technology and channel mixes may have an opportunity for improvement through a marketing operations function. Things like underutilized marketing automation, siloed analytics or conflicts between Sales and Marketing are red flags that indicate a person devoted to marketing operations is needed.

12

Sales Development

For B2B companies, your sales development team can be the heartbeat of your organization. This team is made up of your inbound group, who is responsible for nurturing and converting warm inbound leads (marketing-driven), and your outbound group responsible for cold outbound prospecting. Sometimes, this is a hybrid function where the same people are responsible for both inbound and outbound. The sales development team is usually the first live interaction a potential buyer will have with your organization and it's crucial to the success of your revenue team. Although the sales development team members carry many titles like inbound sales representative (ISR), lead development representative (LDR), sales development representatives (SDR), business development representatives (BDR), account development representatives (ADR), or many others, their purpose is always the same. They will qualify a lead's likelihood of purchasing, determine whether the lead is worth pursuing, and pass ownership to the sales team at some point depending on the handoff process. Their goal is to create pipeline for your sales reps.

Sales or Marketing?

You may be asking yourself why Sales Development is under the Marketing section of this book, Sales Development usually sits under Sales, right? According to the Bridge Group, 65% of sales development teams do reside with the Sales Organization. But it's increasingly common for Sales Development to reside under Marketing, and inbound teams are roughly twice as likely to report to Marketing compared to hybrid or outbound groups. Most of our experience has been with both inbound and outbound teams reporting to Marketing, and it's a structure that has several advantages.

First, the inbound team is the beneficiary of one of Marketing's most precious resources: inbound leads. Having clear communication, both ways, between the inbound team and the marketing team on lead sources and response is super valuable here. The proactive "what's coming next" and "why it's important" type of information to the inbound team, and the feedback of "how it was received" and "how it can be improved" back to the marketing team are basic data but important to collect. While you can certainly get this information across teams, it's likely going to be more complete and easier to collect with inbound and Marketing working collaboratively.

Second, if there are dedicated inbound and outbound reps, consider putting them on the same team. Inbound and outbound reps are measured similarly, require similar training and motivation, and there is plenty of natural career pathing opportunity to leverage between the two groups. As an added benefit, it's easier to manage one team versus two, and the opportunity for cross-learning is significantly higher if in- and outbound reps are in one group.

Third, both inbound and outbound teams should always be leveraging marketing resources like upcoming events, content, campaigns, case studies, etc. While the same can be said for Sales, the main responsibility of Sales Development is qualifying prospects, and the best way to ensure this qualifying is impactful is to have both teams be super close to the marketing calendar.

Finally, as we've iterated over and over, the relationship between Sales and Marketing is really important. Sales Development is an essential bridge between Sales and Marketing and facilitates plenty of healthy collaboration. Sales Development can also serve as a fertile breeding ground for future sales reps, thus making the bridge between the two teams even stronger. It's worth noting that while good sales development reps often make good sales reps (a very common career path), it's not the only path for SDRs. We've seen good sales development reps be successfully promoted to just about every department across an organization including Sales, Marketing, Customer Success, Sales Enablement, Operations, you name it. Except Legal and Engineering! We haven't seen any SDRs go to Legal or Engineering ... yet. A high performing SDR knows how to put in the work, knows the value proposition better than anyone in the organization, knows how to collaborate across teams, and knows how to talk to and convert prospects. What's not to like?

Sales development can live successfully under either Sales or Marketing. Ultimately, ownership of Sales Development should come down to the most capable department, and you should ask the questions, who has the bandwidth, knowledge, and passion to lead this team most effectively?

Leadership

Your Sales Development leader is one role that you absolutely need to get right because the success of the team is dependent upon it. We were fortunate to work with Christy Weymouth, one of the best Sales Development leaders there is, at ExactTarget and Return Path. She embodies the best characteristics of any leader, and the Sales Development teams she builds are world class. Being an SDR is hard, really hard. Grinding it out all day, connecting with one out of 30 calls, and being rejected over and over again will take its toll on anyone. A good SDR leader makes this job exciting, rewarding, and even fun. It requires constant coaching, training, motivation, and celebrating success. A good SDR leader is someone who can communicate effectively across departments, especially Sales, and resolve conflict quickly. Perhaps most importantly, the SDR leader requires someone who can manage a never-ending rotation of individuals moving in, out, and up the organization while still hitting team targets. The onboarding experience for the SDR team needs to be a machine. You'll have to hire quickly, train effectively, and leverage all your resources including your existing team to get new hires to ramp as soon as possible. Then, you'll have to keep them engaged and learning while producing. The onboarding, training, coaching, and other tasks all need to happen during a short period of time before an SDR moves on to their next role. The average tenure of an SDR is about 1½ years, so it's one of the highest turnover departments of every company. Ideally, as noted above, your SDRs are moving on to other roles in the company!

Where to Start

Before you spend the time and resources to start up a sales development team, or before you just "put a person in there," you'll first need to figure out if it's even the right time to start a sales development team. You might not need sales development for some time if, for example, you have the capability to route leads directly to the sales team, or if you can get Sales to spend more time prospecting (which can be really healthy). Take a good look at your sales team and the sales process. How much time are they spending on creating opportunities versus working deals? Is the sales process conducive to a handoff without losing too much momentum? Is your messaging and value proposition solid enough to build a repeatable process and train a new and more junior team to execute? If the answer is yes, it's likely time to start a sales development team.

You'll then need to determine the reporting structure and nature of the role. We suggested that Sales Development can report to Sales or Marketing but remember it's bandwidth, knowledge, and passion that are most important. After you figure out the structure, you'll need to focus on the nature of the role. Here you'll want to consider generating pipeline through inbound lead qualification, outbound prospecting, or a combination of both. You may have enough inbound leads to start there. Or perhaps you'll want to start a dedicated outbound role as well? Or maybe it's a hybrid role that does both? We believe there is power in focus and repetition for this role, and we would suggest dedicated roles, but your business, sales team, and needs will dictate that.

Then, make sure you have alignment with the sales organization. What are the goals and expectations? Is your sales team generating meetings or qualified opportunities? What is the ratio of SDRs to sales reps and how are they aligned (by territory or segment, for example)? What is the handoff process? This one is important. Be sure to build out clear definitions for an official handoff. What is the process, and who is responsible for what if there is a no-show, or if an opportunity isn't quite ready? Shared and consistent processes, goals, and expectations early on will save a lot of headaches down the road. Remember, the success of each team will be dependent upon the other team.

You'll need to finalize compensation plans. This could be a whole chapter in itself, but a base salary plus variable plan based on both number of meetings or opportunities and quality by conversion to pipeline or close is common. Consider a way to incentivize team performance and align with sales success metrics as well. Compensation plans will change as the team and business evolve, so build with that in mind.

You'll need to build your technology to support the team including your CRM, sales productivity tools, call software, and collaboration tools. Define your KPIs. What is the behavior and channels that you expect to be most effective? And by "channels," we mean broadly everything: calls, connects, emails, LinkedIn Inmail, social. You'll likely need to experiment, so be ready to test and measure the effectiveness of each of these over time, and make adjustments based on what is working and what is not.

Building a highly effective sales development team is hard work, but can be so beneficial to your organization in many ways. Strive to build a solid foundation early with the right leadership, and with strong alignment between the company and sales leadership on expectations. With this foundation you will get on the right track. Remember that the work this team does is incredibly hard, and they are often under-appreciated. Invest in training and development, provide them the tools and resources they need to succeed, and celebrate their success. You never know: today's SDR may be your future SVP of Sales!

A Note on Working with Agencies

At some point in your career as a startup CMO, you will find yourself hiring and working with some form of agency: digital, advertising, PR, or some kind of hybrid agency. Agencies can be the biggest boost to your team's capabilities and capacity and drive transformational thinking and work for your marketing efforts. They can also be an enormous waste of time and money.

In days gone by, traditional ad agencies simply charged clients a percentage of their ad spend—and that spend was so large (TV commercials, etc.) that the charge covered all the agency's expenses. PR agencies almost never billed that way and stuck to more of a monthly retainer model. What both of these models have in common is that they were very hard for clients to decipher and trace back value. But as with everything in the last 20 years, all that has changed. If you're a startup working with an agency, you're almost certainly paying them on a "time and materials" basis—and possibly a retainer, but one that is closely tracked back to activities.

Whole books can be written (and have been written!) about working with agencies, so we'll boil down our thinking here to three simple rules we have to maximizing your agency relationship, regardless of the type of agency:

1. **Treat the agency like a close partner or employee.** The more time you invest in the relationship, the more you get out of it. If the people working on your account at an agency are invested in your company and your brand—if they see your quarterly all-hands meetings or your Board Books as if they were a trusted senior member of the team and therefore feel like a trusted senior member of the team—they will do higher quality, more relevant, and likely greater quantity of work for the same price.

2. **Use the agency to gain a fresh perspective.** Even if you follow rule 1 above, your agency team is not, in fact, employed by you

full-time. Even long-term agency relationships rotate people on and off accounts from time to time. You and your permanent team are very close to your brand, your business, and your customers, but that closeness can occasionally be myopic. Listen closely to your agency, even if they are a little bit incorrect in their word choice or assessment of a specific situation. They are taking into account a much broader set of data about the world, with less bias, than you are. About everything.

3. **Use the agency for competencies you can't hire in-house.** Whether those competencies are in a "peak burst" (e.g., you are doing a website redesign which will require 3x your current in-house capacity but only for 3 months), or those competencies come in the form of expensive specialists that you don't need or can't afford on a full-time basis (e.g., brand refresh creative development or crisis management PR team), this flexible use of talent is a much more cost effective and rapid response way to go than hiring full-time talent. If all you're doing is using an agency as an "arms and legs" extension of your team, you are probably paying too much money for too little relative output.

13

Building a Marketing Machine (Scaleup)

As your company transitions from startup to scaleup, your marketing organization should be in lockstep with that evolution. This is the time to build upon the foundation you've laid and level up the work being executed across the marketing team.

Growing Your Team

As your marketing output grows, so will your marketing team. While a startup marketing team may have a few individuals who wear many hats—for example, a single individual who handles both brand design and digital marketing execution—as the need for more marketing work grows, it will be important to identify where responsibilities can be shared and built upon in order to make the team more successful. How to scale your marketing team will be very much driven by the needs of the company and requires the marketing leader to have a pulse on the work being done today as well as where marketing can make more impact in the future. Marketing team growth also depends on the opportunities to increase output with additional people and it depends on the aspirations of the individuals on the existing team. How would they like to spend their time? What are they passionate about and want to dive deeper into? What do they dislike and avoid? All of these elements—company needs and existing marketing team members' needs and skills—factor into the roles you add and how you structure the team.

When it comes to growing your team, it's important to keep in mind that the best talent can be found in unexpected places. One of the great benefits of marketing is that, quite honestly, it isn't rocket science. Most people are pretty well equipped to learn the basic functions of any marketing role. What really sets some marketers apart, however, are the intangible qualities that aren't necessarily honed in marketing-specific roles. Qualities like creative thinking, problem solving, willingness to work outside of title, interest in collaborating, and strong writing and communication skills are not taught in a marketing program, for example, but those are the qualities that make people effective in marketing roles. They're also the qualities that can be found in anybody. So, for example, if you're looking for a content marketer, you don't need to limit yourself to only people with past content marketing experience. Instead, journalists can be a great fit for these roles because of their ability to work against deadlines, communicate complex topics in a concise manner, and write in a variety of different styles or formats.

From personal experience, Holly's career started in video production in a role that was essentially project management. In that role, however, she managed project timelines and budgets, worked directly with customers, managed the workload of team members across multiple projects, and did a lot of storytelling. She didn't know it at the time, but it was all setting her up to be an effective marketer. Luckily, her future boss was able to see that even though she'd never been in "Marketing." She had the right skill set to lead a brand team, essentially launching his true marketing career.

Execute Across Channels

As your team and resources grow, your ability to execute campaigns across channels more seamlessly grows as well. The "omni-channel" experience—having a consistent brand and message "everywhere"—is what every marketing team aspires to create. With limited time, budget, and personnel, sometimes that fully realized vision can be a challenge to achieve As you scale, beginning to elevate the definition of a successful campaign allows you to push your team and your marketing output to new heights.

When you're thinking about a cross-channel campaign, every function of your Marketing team should have a role. More than that, each function should be in full collaboration with every other function, either owning, leading, or contributing to each activity within the campaign. Take a product launch campaign, for example. Your "Go Live" date would align with the chosen launch date of the new product. From that date, your marketing team can plan out everything to happen leading up to, on the day of, and after that date, in order to launch a fully cross-channel campaign. Launch Day may include a new webpage, email marketing campaigns triggered to customers, prospects, and partners; it might include the launch of new blog content and/or thought leadership content, promotional messages across social channels, coordinated outreach to prospects from the sales development team; it might also include a training webinar for current customers, and an in-person event in a key market. All of these activities would then be tracked back to a centralized dashboard with KPIs to measure engagement and impact across audiences and channels.

The centralized dashboard with KPIs

At Return Path, while we took an omni-channel approach to every product launch, our most exciting, collaborative, and far-reaching campaigns were often our annual brand campaigns. We weren't promoting a specific new product or offering, but we were focused on driving brand awareness and evolving our brand at least once per year. These campaigns required close collaboration across all functions of the marketing team, coordinating content launches, one-to-one and one-to-many outreach, in-person and virtual events, and new digital experiences. These campaigns allowed each function within Marketing to shine independently while being supported by the work of all the other functions, and they truly demonstrated that the whole is more than the sum of its parts.

Not only were these brand campaigns exciting challenges for our marketing team, they had a significant impact on Marketing's overarching goal of driving pipeline and bookings. Each year our data showed that these campaigns generated a substantial number of new leads, influenced revenue within existing business, and consistently increased brand awareness. In fact, our 2016 campaign delivered a 10% increase in brand awareness over our 2015 campaign.

Broaden Your Reach

If you've scaled Marketing in lockstep with your company, you've added significant talent to your team, you're firing on all cylinders with your campaign launches, and you're seeing quantifiable results between marketing and revenue. What comes next? Global expansion. If your scaleup is already moving at the pace to be making significant marketing investment and seeing that investment pay off through innovative, successful marketing campaigns, chances are that global expansion is already a topic of conversation at the executive level.

When it comes to breaking into new markets, localization is key. And we don't just mean translating your English content into French, Spanish, German, or other languages. Each market is unique, with their own cultures, ways of doing business, and processes for evaluating purchases. It's critical for your business and your marketing team to have a presence in-market to influence what needs to shift from your existing US-centric approach to be successful in a new region. Here are a few ways a marketer in your target regions can positively impact global expansion.

- **Accurate translation.** Google Translate certainly won't cut it, and even a stellar translation agency can still fall short. It's hugely important to have a resource in-market who can ensure that all the hard work you've put into developing a particular brand voice makes sense in an entirely different language. A qualified local person can also help ensure that your brand and message are applied consistently across campaigns and channels, in the same way you'd expect consistency across your English language work.

- **Local examples.** Most global markets don't just want to hear about the great work you've done in North America. You may have to start there as an entry point, but it will be key to get local examples as soon as possible. Local examples will help significantly in gaining legitimacy in the region and demonstrate your awareness of their particular challenges, beyond just their business size, industry, or business challenge.

- **Cultural insight.** An event that works for a French audience won't necessarily work for a Brazilian one, and vice versa. Not only is it important to have a local resource who can provide insight into what works or what doesn't, it's equally important to *trust* that person to do what they know to be right. Forcing an approach onto a region because it worked in the US or in another country won't necessarily breed repeatable success. Instead, it could work against you and highlight a lack of understanding of them, their country, and their culture.

III. CMO AND THE LEADERSHIP TEAM

14

Collaborating With The Leadership Team

Nick Badgett and Holly Enneking

We've talked a lot about marketing and collaboration. Marketing requires deep collaboration with all other functional leaders. Sales, Product, Customer Success, Finance, Business Development, HR—you name it and Marketing plays a key role. These departments and leaders understand the value of Marketing and they've experienced the benefits of having a deep partnership with Marketing. For example, customer marketing and partner marketing focus will only happen with deep collaboration with your Chief Customer Officer and Head of Partnerships. The customer and partner marketing manager positions themselves may come to fruition in the first place because these individuals identify the need. Individuals who perform these roles may report to Marketing, but spend a significant amount of time with the customer or partner team. This isn't going to work unless the leaders are on the same page, and are collaborating regularly and efficiently. In today's fast-changing and largely digital world, other functional areas realize that they need

Marketing to be successful. And it works both ways: the marketing department is only as healthy as its relationships with other teams. Because Marketing is critical across the organization, the marketing leader will have first-hand knowledge and a deep understanding of priorities across the company. We get to see the "bigger picture" when it may not be so obvious for others to see. We also have the opportunity to extend the reach of an initiative across departmental aisles, to broaden the scope of a campaign, or to surface the success of an otherwise isolated idea, often resulting in a snowball effect. The marketing leader has a big seat at the executive table, and a unique perspective that can add value in multiple ways.

Also, remember that Marketing is a shared service and can sometimes make the biggest impact when acting in service to the rest of the company. No, we're not suggesting that we're order takers, but we can lead the charge of demonstrating what healthy collaboration looks like. And we're in the perfect position to do so. Today's marketers are creative but also analytical and methodical, we're both left-brained and right-brained. We're responsible for the company's brand, generating demand, and for helping to maintain a healthy culture. It's impossible to do this alone. As the CMO, you'll want to start establishing healthy relationships with leadership, continue building healthy relationships throughout the rest of the organization, and demonstrate how to collaborate broadly to your team so that they do the same. Finger pointing is not an option.

What I Look For in a Chief Marketing Officer

Let's get this out of the way: I despise the word "marketing"— it's often the weakest link in a startup company. "Marketing" is vague and non-specific, often poorly executed and measured, and usually a colossal waste of money relative to the output. There are plenty of classical approaches that any marketing consultant would be happy to charge you lots of money to explain. However, practical marketing strategies have evolved in the past decade, especially as user-generated content, online marketing, and the idea of building a brand have become ubiquitous.

For a while, I asserted that marketing was all about "thought leadership," prompted by an email from my business partner, Chris Moody, who wrote:

Don't do marketing. Focus on becoming a thought leader in your space. Talk every day with your customers, prospective customers, partners, and the world about why you do what you do and why you think it is important. The reality is you can only talk about what you do one or two times before people think "got it" and stop listening. But, if you talk about what you believe and point to countless examples that exemplify your beliefs, you can build real engagement with people who care/believe the same things.

Would I look for a Chief Marketing Officer who is a "thought leader?" Nope. That term, like "user-generated content," has become omnipresent and the meaning diluted. How many thought leaders are there anyway? While you can probably find one, they aren't going to manage your marketing organization at scale. Instead, look for someone with a point of view that can resist the marketing fad of the day. They should be driven by an obsessive focus on the customer and the product, rather than a marketing budget, initiative, or brand. If the person you are talking to about the role leads with phrases like "social media marketing" and "marketing spend," or talks about "refreshing your brand," be skeptical.

Instead of talking about marketing, a CMO should focus their energy on your customer and your product. They should be a key, integrated part of your leadership team, working side by side with your CRO and your CPO because many tactical marketing initiatives are regularly changing. Any CMO can manage a team executing them. The great CMOs understand why your customers care about what you do, and they talk to them more than anyone else. **Brad Feld, *Foundry Group Partner, Techstars Cofounder***

15

How to Hire a Chief Marketing Officer

Nick Badgett and Holly Enneking

At some point in the life of your startup you'll have to hire a Chief Marketing Officer. While we can't give you an exact metric to tell you when to hire a CMO, it will most likely be one of a few scenarios. The first is rapid growth and increased complexity of marketing. Maybe someone from your internal marketing team is not yet ready to step into the C-suite, or maybe you don't have the time to nurture someone and help them develop the skills necessary to be CMO. With the increased complexity and demand for experience, an outside hire may be what you need. A second, and something we wrote about earlier (see Chapter 3), is when it's time for a refresh. They need to re-brand, reintroduce themselves to the market, break up the old way of thinking, and generate fresh ideas and a common way to do that is to hire a new CMO. On the flipside, if your marketing is ineffective, if you're not getting the ROI you want, if you have a lot of attrition or poor engagement within the team, hiring an outside CMO makes a lot of sense.

Regardless of whether you want to hire a CMO because of increased complexity, or you need fresh ideas, or your marketing just isn't effective, there are several things to think about before you start looking at resumes or working with an executive search firm. One way we think about the CMO role is to think in terms of the skills and attributes a person will bring with them. We believe there are four distinct *personas* that define the vast majority of marketers: brand, growth, product, and influence marketers., Each are relatively distinct and cohesive so that people in one *persona* will be similar to all others in that *persona* but different from people in the other *personas.* By the time you get to the CMO level, you are obviously familiar with the totality of marketing, but each person will have preferences, values, and deeper experience in one *persona* rather than deep experience in all of them. Choosing the right CMO for your startup depends on finding a person with the skills and *attributes* that will make a big impact moving forward. So, if you're a B2C startup, someone within the brand or influence *persona,* might be a better choice than someone who has experience in B2B and product marketing.

Persona Attributes and How to Find Them

Nearly every CMO will have familiarity with brand marketing since branding applies to every company, startup and mature, and companies selling B2B and B2C. But, if a person specializes in branding you ought to see multiple messages (either written on their resume or heard when you interview them) highlighting their skills. For example, a brand marketer will not only focus on building brand awareness and affinity for the brand, but they will also be skilled at developing the overall brand. That development of the brand will include the message, the look, and the feel. In their day-to-day tasks a brand marketer will be focused on supporting the internal culture development, employee engagement, and recruitment.

If you're looking on LinkedIn, another platform, or using an executive recruiter to find your next CMO you should look for people who have a track record of working with brand, digital, have a content marketing background, or people who started their career in a creative/ad agency role. Another thing to look for are references to storytelling, messaging, or work with global brands. Finally, a brand marketer may reference creating digital and in-person experiences as part of their skill set.

Someone within the growth *persona* will have deep experience and skills in attracting demand and moving prospects through the sales funnel. A growth marketer will also be more quantitative than other *personas* so they will often be data driven and analytically minded, and they will be adept at testing and iterating. On LinkedIn or other platforms, people in the growth *persona* will have a track record involving digital marketing, demand generation, or a marketing operations background. They may also have interaction with sales development or experience in an SDR/BDR or sales role. Either on their resume or in conversations during an interview, a growth marketer will make references to ABM, GTM, or building/managing a tech stack.

A product *persona* is typical of a marketer who is highly technical but also able to translate technologies and complex information into digestible messaging. A product marketer will have deep market skills and will understand personas, competitors, and market needs and they will be well versed in pricing, packaging, and positioning. On their resume or LinkedIn you ought to see a background in product marketing or sales enablement and references to alignment with product and sales.

The influence *persona* is primarily marketers who are relationship and engagement driven. An influence marketer will thrive on being out in front of people, either directly in face-to-face interactions or in the spotlight presenting or speaking. The influence marketer will be comfortable as the brand evangelist both within the company and externally to multiple stakeholders. On LinkedIn or on their resume, the influence marketer will have a strong personal brand that may include public speaking, a social media presence, personal website, podcast, or published written materials. Often, the influence marketer has experience in content marketing or field marketing.

When Is The Right Time For This *Persona*?

Earlier we said that we can't give you an exact metric that will let you know when to hire your CMO, but we can provide some ideas on what your company may be experiencing that would lead to a CMO hire for each *persona*. It might be time to consider a brand marketer if your business needs to build brand recognition or even create a new category. After a merger or an acquisition a brand marketer will help to create a consistent message to the outside world, and they can also help if your business needs to pivot. Additionally, a brand marketer can be key if your business needs to attract talent within your industry or space. In short, if your company needs to increase brand awareness and visibility then a brand marketer *persona* is the right choice for your next CMO.

On the other hand, if you are an early-stage company primed to scale quickly then a growth marketer *persona* may be exactly what you need. A growth marketer can help if your business has reached product/market fit and you are ready to quickly scale demand. A growth marketer is also the right type of CMO to go after if you find your company in a crowded, established market and you need to attract customers. A product market *persona* is often the best choice when a company is early stage, wants to scale, but is working to find product/market fit. If your company is scaling from a single product or a few first successful products to a platform/suite of products and you are doing that either organically or through an acquisition, a product marketer can be the way to go. With product-led growth and the detailed data analytics needed, the product CMO is often the right person to lead the marketing team.

Finally, an influence marketer *persona* is often a good choice for CMO if a company is later stage and moving toward an IPO. Companies at this stage often need a larger team to push execution around the vision and a CMO that can be the external face (potentially in place of a founder) can make a big impact on the company.

General Interview Questions

Although we have identified four *personas* in marketing that ought to serve you well in hiring your first (or next) CMO, there are some general questions you can ask each CMO candidate. For example, if you ask the question, "Marketing is a blend of art and science; where do your strengths lie within the spectrum of marketing activity?" you ought to hear different answers based on the *persona*. For example, a brand marketer will most likely focus on storytelling, brand building, and cultivating the culture within the organization. The growth marketer might mention things around digital marketing, growth hacking, and data analysis. A product marketer answering that question would focus on understanding the customer, product/market fit, or collaborating deeply with the product organization. And you should expect to hear answers from the influence marketer that their focus is getting in front of clients and prospects, evangelizing the product and leading a team.

Similarly, if you ask each *persona* the question, "What are key KPIs you typically track against?" you should hear different responses. A brand marketer, for example, might list KPIs involving impressions, ad engagement, traffic, leads, or press and social media coverage. The growth marketer and product marketer will have KPIs around leads and conversion rates and the product marketer might also mention feature adoption as a KPI they track. Finally, the influence marketer will focus on KPIs that involve page views, downloads, and follows.

Other general questions that we found helpful to understand CMO candidates include:

- I know there are several paths you can come up in marketing, help me understand you as a marketer - What do you own? What don't you own from a marketing standpoint?

- When you first joined the company, what did the marketing organization look like? Were there existing processes in place? What was the company doing from a marketing perspective before you joined?

- What are some of the big marketing initiatives you drove while at ___?

- Where is your bread and butter as a marketer and where would you hire strong people around you?

- How do you acquire new customers?

- How metrics-driven is your organization?

- What is your marketing budget? Where is most of your spend directed?

- How much of your business is online vs. offline? How is your product sold?

- What was the go-to-market launch strategy and were you the person to lead that process? How did it change for successive products/launches under your watch?

- Do you have established relationships with partners? What types of companies do you partner with?

- How does content play into your marketing strategy and do you have an expert on your team leading this initiative or is it out-sourced to any agency?

- Do you have experience marketing overseas?

Quantitative Marketing Questions

- What techniques are you using on the social marketing front? How do you measure results?

- What Analytical Tools are you using? How do you measure and track your marketing programs?

- What does the marketing conversion funnel look like for the company?

- Does the company have a monetization strategy? How much of that is the responsibility of marketing vs. sales, business development and operations leadership?

- Do you work closely with product or engineering? (only ask this if you need someone who specifically has this DNA) How closely involved are you with defining product strategy and changing the product to deliver better results in marketing?

Brand Marketing Questions:

- What is the branding strategy there? Do you invest or have a budget or team that focuses in offline marketing initiatives, such as PR, events, TV, print advertising, in-store retail promotions or partners/sponsorship?

- What channels have been the strongest performing? Which were your weakest?

- Is there an in-house creative team? Who do you use as your agency of record?

Although there are a number of questions beyond the one listed here, finding the right CMO involves understanding your company well, understanding the markets in which you compete and the customers you sell to, and understanding the *persona* that best matches the impact you hope to make. Unlike some of the other executive hires a company can make, the CMO role is much broader, and marketing touches nearly everything in a company—the culture, values, vision, product, people, customers, and perception. It is both quantitative and qualitative; it involves all forms of communication. While you may not be able to find a CMO that checks off every box, at least two qualities are vitally important. First, because of the complexity and rapidly changing landscape of marketing, a person who is intellectually curious and open to change will be able to thrive in nearly any situation. Second, because marketing touches nearly everything inside and outside of a company, a person who believes in collaboration will ultimately be more successful and impactful than people who view marketing as a silo.

16

Fractional Chief Marketing Officer

Scott Kabat

I've worked in every stage of a company from cofounding a two-person Y Combinator education technology company up to being acquired by Cisco and working in their enormous machine. I'm a firm believer that every company will need a fully functioning marketing team, and it's important to figure out, when you factor in hiring time and budgets, what the right prioritization of the full-time roles are. And then you need to think about where you can supplement those people with senior guidance or boots on the ground so they can get more done. The fractional CMO can be an extremely valuable option for some companies, especially startups and scaleups.

Fractional Opportunities for CMOs

There's a big need for fractional CMOs and it's largely driven by the fast-paced changing nature of marketing. My experience, and one that I think a lot of CMOs are experiencing—especially in late-stage startups—is that invariably you eventually hit a point where the strategy changes. The needs of the organization change and you realize that you're not right for the company anymore. And for a lot of CMOs, their tenure with a company is 6–18 months and then they're back in the job hunting market. I didn't want to cycle in and out all the time and the fractional role allows me to be in market rather than in between jobs. I started doing fractional CMO work almost exclusively with startups that had raised some capital, launched a product or were about to, but didn't know a lot about marketing, and frankly, weren't at the point where they needed to hire an expensive full-time CMO. I found that there was a real opportunity not only for startups but also for later stage companies going through big strategic transitions with a change in business model, or a private equity firm investing in an old line business to digitally transform it.

My experience in fractional roles comes in two different flavors and I always seem to have a composite of each. There's the kind of fractional CMO where you're running the marketing team on a limited basis, which I generally do no more than two days a week with one company. And I spread that time allocation through the week. And then there's the advisory CMO which is generally when the company is already executing and my job is to weigh in and give guidance. In the advisory-type role, we have a weekly rhythm of checking in but operationally I am less involved. It's worth noting that especially in marketing there are different approaches to being a fractional CMO. Some people have a standard assessment and playbook and they run you through their analysis, usually with a particular emphasis on performance marketing and the client side of it. I generally operate more as a full stack and I'll say to a company, "Let's look across the mix at both the client side and the softer side and figure out what's right for that company." Different people approach it differently.

In some respects, your role as a fractional is the same as if you were full-time. You are still leading from the front on strategy and working with key stakeholders, with the executive team and Board, and within the marketing team to put a plan and strategy together. You're still looking ahead to what's coming and creating a roadmap, which is actually really important for startups. It's common in a startup to get so into the weeds that you're not looking at where the step function changes need to happen. So those tasks—creating a strategy and a roadmap, are the same in either a fractional or full-time role.

The biggest difference is really figuring out the line between your role as a fractional and the business. You have to be able to back off and understand that this is their thing. I will give advice and drive solutions and guide them but at the end of the day I'm not a part of the team and I have to back off at certain points. I generally try to work as an embedded member of the team so I err more on being integral rather than being hands off. But, because you're not really a full-fledged member of the team, that's different. And then, obviously, I will get involved in a lot of the people and the organizational dynamics but I'm not writing performance reviews, I'm not managing the operational back end of leading a team as an executive.

I believe there is a lot of opportunity for fractional CMOs, but it's not the same as full-time and it might not be for everyone, especially if you need to be highly involved and control the entire marketing team.

Qualities of a Fractional CMO

It's critical for the fractional CMO to see the big picture at all times. Where I'm catching startups is when they've raised a round of funding, they just sold a dream, and there's this temptation to want to do it all. And part of where I try to add some perspective is, "Hey, guys, let's look ahead to what the next big milestone is, maybe it's the next funding round or the next product launch that's a little further down the road. Let's develop a prioritized plan to get there." So, a key skill is to maintain a degree of objectivity and to view the bigger picture through a strategic lens.

Another key skill is being able to context shift because I'm generally working with multiple companies, sometimes with five at a time. And during the course of any given day, I'll have a meeting for one client, a call for another and back and forth. I find it stimulating and I've noticed that the pattern recognition has sharpened my toolset as a marketer. But it can be dizzying at times. There is another model where some people work full-time four days a week, but I have steered clear of that. I generally work no more than one and a half or two days a week with one company.

The other skill that is critical I mentioned earlier, and that's the ability to be able to walk the line between speaking with conviction and adapting within the existing organism of the culture. No one is hiring you to be a fractional executive to just keep the trains running on time. But at the same time, it's not the sort of role that works well if you're just a bull in a china shop. I don't think there's any way I could be successful at this if I hadn't had deep experience as an operator and dealing with all the messiness of making the sausage because you have to appreciate that. And things go sideways with these businesses all the time, so I spend a lot of time reassuring them like, "Hey don't worry about this, I've seen it before and it's okay. We're here to help."

One thing I really liked about being an operator that I've tried to hold on to as a fractional is the chance to mentor and advise people. Because particularly in startups, this work is very personal and I enjoy being able to guide startups through the journey. That's not really a skill or a quality you need to be a successful fractional CMO, but the bigger point is to find what you like doing and bring that to every situation.

Fractional Opportunities for Companies

When I talk to CEOs, they'll say to me, "Look, I have to decide if I'm going to do this fractional thing or hire someone." I don't see that as an either-or scenario because what I generally see, particularly when it comes to hiring a head of marketing, is that there are 1,000 different flavors of marketers these days and if you don't know exactly what you need, what the musts are, and what the wants are, and how it fits into where the business could go, can you really hire someone? People might not last long or the process of hiring might take much longer than you think.

A fractional CMO can help you through that process and help you think about the job profile, help you vet candidates, help to onboard and advise those new hires so that it shrinks their time to impact. In a world where the CMO's tenure can be very short, you can't really afford to have someone come in and get a slow start. So, one role of a fractional, one benefit to the high growth company, is that this person can get involved upstream to assist with finding, vetting, and onboarding a full-time CMO. The fractional CMO can help them through when they start and then eventually recede into the background and support those hires with operational risks. It's rarely as much of an either-or thing as people think.

17

CEO-to-CEO Advice About the Marketing Role

Matt Blumberg

What comes before a full-fledged CMO? In most startups, there is at least a medium-sized and quite busy marketing department with multiple mid-level leaders well before there is a seasoned leader at the helm. One of those leaders may be a VP of Marketing—depending on the nature of the company, it is likely someone with a specialized area of focus within Marketing (brand, digital, event, etc.) who has some working knowledge of the other areas.

Signs It's Time to Hire Your First CMO

You know it's time to hire a CMO when:

- You wake up in the middle of the night concerned that no one in your company but you knows how to orchestrate a successful product launch.

- You are spending too much of your own time managing smaller pieces of marketing because your marketing leader isn't experienced enough across all of the function's many sub-disciplines.

- Your Board asks you how you would spend an extra $2m in marketing if you had it—or what you'd cut if you had to reduce your marketing spend by 50%, and you don't have a great answer and aren't sure how to get to one.

When a Fractional CMO Might Be Enough

A fractional CMO may be the way to go, if you have a generalist marketing manager or director who has strategic inclinations but not enough experience operating as a strategic executive and who just needs a little more supervision in order to "level up." Or if you have a series of more junior leaders of marketing sub-functions, none of whom is experienced enough to coordinate activities across groups but none of whom require a full-time leader.

What Does Great Look Like in a CMO?

Ideal startup CMOs do four things particularly well:

1. They understand that the marketing budget starts with drivers and business results and works backwards in a modular way to spend, not the other way around. They understand what the business needs to achieve—the sales plan—then what the funnel looks like. Then they know what marketing levers they can pull to both optimize the funnel and make sure the funnel is full. And they build the plan in a modular way so that if the budget needs to be trimmed, they can ask the right questions and easily trim it.

2. They make spend decisions on data, not on a hunch or because

"that's what's always worked." Even in traditional B2C businesses that make heavy use of traditional non-addressable media like print, outdoor, and TV—today, everything can be tested and measured to some degree. A strong CMO is one who starts every answer with "Let's look at the data."

3. They behave like a CEO in terms of being able to orchestrate the different pieces and parts of their organization. Just as a CEO has to manage a litany of disparate functions, so too do CMOs have to manage a litany of disparate channels. Gone are the days when CMOs were either "brand or direct" or "online or offline." Today, the average CMO has to be able to manage 20+ different channels. The level of complexity and number of points of failure for the job have exploded. A great CMO handles this with the fluidity that the CEO handles moving from a sales pipeline meeting to a product road-mapping exercise.

4. They spend time in-market and in-product. Given all the responsibilities around multi-channel orchestration, systems, budgeting, and execution in general, it can be very easy for a CMO to operate 100% from behind the desk. The great ones want—need—to be out in the field, attending sales calls, partner meetings, events, serving as executive sponsor on some key accounts, in general, collecting primary data on the company's products and brand.

Signs Your CMO Isn't Scaling

CMOs who aren't scaling well past the startup stage are the ones who typically:

- Treat all tasks like French fries (see the *What is Marketing, Really?* textbox). Wait, what? Marketing can easily be a service center as opposed to a strategic function. I don't think that's ideal, but that may be how a company decides to run it. You're never too full to eat one more French fry. You may be too full to order a plate of fries, but not one more individual, tasty, crunchy, salty, fry. Marketing at its worst can be the same. There's always one more task to be done on the long list of tasks. CMOs who focus on task execution (eating the next fry) and can't pull up to think about whether they're doing the right thing (should they be ordering another plate of fries?) are simply not scaling.

- Report on activity as opposed to outcome. This is related to my prior point. When all the world is a task list, then report-outs are just volumes of tasks. I'm not sure why Marketing ended up like this, but it's frequently the only function in the company that spends time producing beautiful reports on all the stuff they do. It probably comes from years of working with agencies who report like that to justify client spend. Regardless, can you imagine seeing reports on activity instead of outcomes from other departments? The report from the CFO that talks about how many collections calls the team made as opposed to reporting on bad debt—no, thank you. The report from the CRO talking about how many meetings a rep had with no mention of pipeline or closes—seriously? CMOs who can't link activity to outcome with a focus on outcome are not scaling with the job.

- Spend disproportionate amounts of time on creative or agency work. That's the glamorous and fun part of marketing, for sure. Having made TV commercials as a head of marketing when I was at MovieFone, I can attest to that. But even if you're a big B2C marketer with a lot of agency and creative spend, while you should be supervising that work, spending all your time on it is a sign that you're not interested in all the other, well, French fries.

How I Engage with the CMO

A few ways I've typically spent the most time or gotten the most value out of CMOs over the years are:

- With the rest of my go-to-market executives as a group, not in a silo. This is even more important than it is with respect to other GTM roles like Sales, Account Management, and Partnerships. While of course I have always had one-to-one meetings with my CMO, I find that the most valuable conversations are the ones with the GTM group as a group, talking about shared objectives and the underlying drivers and coordination points to get there.

- Thinking sessions where we take time away from the day-to-day to do deep dives on strategic topics like the company's positioning, voice, or brand. Sometimes I like to do these in the context of reading a relevant marketing book or business journal article, sometimes not. I find that the most creative thinking and ideas—and even the quantitative part of marketing involves a lot of creativity—happen in some of these longer form, unstructured conversations.

- Before they become the CMO. For years, we went through CMOs at Return Path at the same clip as other companies—one to two years—and we had a pattern of hiring them in from the outside. Over time, though, we realized that we would be much better served by having more continuity in Marketing by grooming people and promoting them from within. The last few CMOs we had at Return Path were all promoted into the role—so I got to know them pretty extensively ahead of time and was not only thrilled to give them a shot at the top job but I was in a great place to understand their strengths and weaknesses coming into the role so I could most effectively mentor them. The same could be said of other functional departments, but Marketing is more acute, based on the average tenure of CMOs.

18

Conclusion

From organizing a marketing team, to tactical execution, to collaborating across the business, we've covered a lot of ground. Whether you're a marketer, a marketing leader, a current CMO, an aspiring CMO, or even in an entirely different role but suspect marketing might be for you, hopefully you've found something valuable here to take away with you. Marketing, when it's done right and taken seriously, can be a game changer for a business, especially a startup. We've witnessed first-hand at multiple companies what Marketing can do to shape a company, drive revenue, and impact how the business evolves.

So, what is marketing, really? Marketing is everything. Marketing is the big ideas and the small actions. The art of the possible and the science of the attainable. The pretty pictures and the cold, hard facts. It can and should impact every part of your business. Sometimes that influence is big, and sometimes it's small, but there is always a role marketing can play to advocate for the customer, bring different perspectives together, drive the narrative of the business, and both define and deliver the promise of your company.

That makes marketing an incredibly exciting place to be. One of the true joys of marketing is that the possibilities are endless. There are countless best practices to follow and proven ways to get the job done, but also a million sideroads you can take or small changes you can make to do something more efficiently, inject more creativity, or reimagine it entirely. With an unending stream of new technologies, creative talent,

and innovative experiences out in the world, marketers are the benefi-
ciaries of a world full of inspiration.

If we can leave you with one final piece of advice, it's this: Marketing
should be fun. If it's not, you're doing something wrong. Yes, there are
goals (sometimes big goals) to hit, like generating opportunities, pipeline,
and revenue. These are critical to the business and the primary objective.
But at its core, marketing is about creating connections.

We are real people creating real relationships with other real people.
The human element is undeniable in everything we do. Lucky for us, no
one's lives are in danger if an email goes to the wrong list or a research
report falls flat. We can fix, update, replace, or remove our mistakes in
pretty short order. Without that pressure, we're able to create an environment within our marketing teams to foster freedom and creativity.
Marketers will always do their best work when they're having fun. If you
can create a space where the goals are clear but the pathway there is
open to debate, where all input is welcome and no ideas are bad ideas,
and where everyone can bring the best they have to offer to the table
while continuing to improve in areas for growth, you'll have created the
perfect environment for marketing magic to happen.

Acknowledgements

This book is derivative of *Startup CXO* and the acknowledgments for this book extends to the people who helped in that effort. The list of people to thank for their role in helping create that is long and has to start with my current and former colleagues who were the primary contributors: Jack Sinclair, Cathy Hawley, Shawn Nussbaum, Ken Takahashi, Nick Badgett, Holly Enneking, Anita Absey, George Bilbrey, Dennis Dayman, and Dave Wilby. *Startup CXO* was a truly collaborative work and the same is true with this book. Cathy and I collaborated together and also with Pete Birkeland, who edited the second edition of *Startup CEO*, was a tireless collaborator for *Startup CXO*, and helped bring this book to fruition.

I would also like to acknowledge the rest of the Bolster team and board that made this possible, especially this book's project manager, Rachel Henry. It wasn't easy to carve out the time to write while scaling up Bolster, much less doing the bulk of the writing over the holidays and I'm grateful to all the contributors for their effort.

Although the professional lives of the contributors are now primarily at Bolster, most of us worked together for many years at Return Path, and all of us would like to thank our Board and shareholders, particularly Fred Wilson, Greg Sands, Scott Weiss, Scott Petry, Jeff Epstein, and Brad Feld (more on Brad in a minute) for giving us the opportunity to learn on the job as we scaled ourselves and scaled the business over the better part of two decades. That experience is what led us to be able to write *Startup CXO*. We'd also like to thank all 1,300 colleagues from Return Path over the years who challenged, inspired, and taught us things every day. Although he was not a Return Path or Bolster team member, Marc Maltz from Hoola Hoop Consulting, my long-time partner as an executive coach, has shaped the thinking of me and of a number of the contributors to this effort.

Startup CXO is part of the *Startup Revolution* series that was created by my long-time board member and friend Brad Feld. Brad's advice on all things business, personal, and writing has been invaluable for over 20 years and whether attributed or not, many of the ideas in this book are the result of many thoughtful conversations with him. I would also like to thank the team at Wiley (Bill Falloon and Purvi Patel) for their help and support as editors, publishers, and marketers.

Startup CXO had a very large number of people who contributed their insights to the final form, which carries over to this book, including sidebars by Rob Krolik and Jeff Epstein, Guy Turner, Greg Sands, Scott Petry, Brad Feld, Dave Wilby, and Scott Dorsey. We are also grateful for the contribution to our fractional chapter from Courtney Graeber.

We received a number of thoughtful comments on specific functional areas from Rick Buck, Caroline Pearl, Diana Caleroni, Jen Goldman, Mike Mutone, Debby Meredith, and Chad Shinsato. Brad Feld and Scott Dorsey did a final read-through of the entire book (not a small feat!) and provided helpful suggestions to the final work.

I want to end by thanking my family for their unwavering support as I embarked on a series of books while scaling a second startup—a combination that I can't exactly endorse as being sane or smart. *Startup CXO* was a collaborative effort but I would have been the anchor holding us back if it weren't for my wife of over two decades, Mariquita. My thanks start and end with her. An executive coach for startup CEOs, Mariquita has been intimately involved in all my professional projects, providing advice, encouragement, and support to whatever I'm doing.

Matt Blumberg

About the Authors

Matt Blumberg. Matt has spent his entire career creating startups, scaling them, and sharing best practices of what works and what doesn't work for other CEOs and team members in the entrepreneurial community. He is the author of *Startup CEO: A Field Guide to Scaling Up Your Business* (Wiley, 2020), an influential book embraced by entrepreneurs, CEOs, founders, and board of directors in the entrepreneurial ecosystem. Startup CEO was an outgrowth of his blog, StartupCEO.com. In 1999, he founded Return Path, an innovative email marketing company, helped it to $100m in revenues, and led it to a successful exit in a strategic sale to Validity in 2019. Along with colleagues from Return Path, Matt started Bolster in 2020, a company focused on helping startups and scaleups grow, develop, and scale their leadership teams and boards. Matt's second book, *Startup CXO: A Field Guide to Scaling Up Your Company's Critical Functions and Teams* (Wiley, 2021), was a collaboration with Bolster's CXOs to provide a blueprint for scaling up each function.

Before Return Path, Matt led Marketing, Product Management, and the Internet Group for MovieFone, Inc. (later acquired by AOL). Prior to that, he served as an associate with private equity firm General Atlantic Partners and was a consultant with Mercer Management Consulting. He also cofounded and chairs the board of Path Forward, a nonprofit created and spun out of Return Path. Path Forward's mission is to empower people to restart their careers after time spent focused on caregiving by working with companies offering mid-career internships. Path Forward gives women and men a path to a professional career, while giving companies access to a diverse, untapped talent force. Matt is currently Executive Chair at Bolster. He earned his A.B. from Princeton University.

Nick Badgett. Nick is an experienced marketing and revenue leader with more than 20 years of experience working in both startup and enterprise environments across the B2B SaaS, telecom, and financial services industries. His approach to marketing has been shaped by experience in a variety of go-to-market roles including sales, sales support, sales development and marketing. Nick collaborated on *Startup CXO: A Field Guide to Scaling Up Your Company's Critical Functions and Teams* (Wiley, 2021), sharing key insights on scaling up the marketing function. Before joining Bolster, Nick held marketing leadership positions with Emplify, Return Path, Salesforce, and ExactTarget. Nick is a cofounder of Bolster, where he currently helps lead the revenue teams. He holds a bachelor's degree in marketing and a master's degree in information & communication sciences, both from Ball State University.

Holly Enneking. Holly is an experienced marketing leader who loves building effective teams and powerful brands to meaningfully impact the growth of a company. Holly is currently the Head of Marketing & Partnerships at Bolster, and thrives on amplifying the Bolster brand and helping executives continually up-level themselves and their teams. Holly contributed to *Startup CXO: A Field Guide to Scaling Up Your Company's Critical Functions and Teams* (Wiley, 2021), sharing her experience, tips, and best practices for CMOs to scale up the marketing function. Prior to Bolster, Holly built the Marketing & Alliances team at Lev, a marketing consultancy focused on Salesforce Marketing Cloud, and ran brand and digital marketing at Return Path, a global software company. She originally began her career in video and digital production before making the move into tech. She earned a BA in communication from DePauw University.